The
Sheltered
Garden

The Sheltered Garden

Alan Toogood

Photographs by John Glover

DAVID & CHARLES
Newton Abbot · London

FRONTISPIECE

*A superb example of a herbaceous border which is well
protected by an ornamental wall. Traditionally
herbaceous borders have a backing of some kind – often
a dark green hedge. Such protection prevents tall
border plants from being battered by wind*
(COMPTON ACRES, DORSET)

British Library Cataloguing in Publication Data
Toogood, Alan R., 1941 –
    The sheltered garden.
    1. Gardening
    I. Title
    635

ISBN 0-7153-9334-0

Text and illustrations © Alan Toogood 1989
Photographs © John Glover 1989

Typeset and designed by John Youé
on a Macintosh system
and printed in Portugal
for David & Charles Publishers plc
Brunel House Newton Abbot Devon

Contents

Introduction

These days gardening authors are not often able to say they have produced an original work, as most subjects have been written about before; many frequently. However, as far as we know *The Sheltered Garden* is unique.

As one might suppose from the title, this book is concerned with protecting gardens from cold winds, so that a much wider range of plants can be grown. The book is not, however, devoted exclusively to totally sheltered gardens, or those which are to be made so. It is also highly relevant to people who have, or who want, sheltered areas within their gardens.

The term shelter applies to features as diverse as warm sunny walls to shade with moist soil under trees. In between are included fragrant areas, sitting areas, wildlife habitats, garden rooms or conservatories, and fruit and vegetable plots. The book will, we hope, be useful to those people who want to create different habitats or atmospheres within the garden, whether it is large or small, on a balcony or on a roof.

NOTE ON ABBREVIATIONS

One especially useful feature of this book is the plant hardiness zone system, to enable you to choose plants that are suitable for your part of the country. Each plant is given a zone number, eg (Z8). This system is fully explained in Chapter 3.

A very popular aspect of gardening today is growing plants in containers, for example, around the house and on patios. Roof and balcony gardeners, of course, appreciate the value of pots, troughs, urns, window boxes and so on. Therefore, we have indicated, throughout the book, often with (c), which plants are suitable for growing in containers. Do not be surprised to learn that these include shrubs, small trees, climbers, roses, fruits and vegetables.

We hope this book will inspire you to create a tranquil haven for both plants and people.

Alan Toogood and John Glover

Courtyards are typical examples of secluded, well-sheltered areas and have been popular since ancient times, especially in warm or hot climates. Well planted, ideally with exotic-looking subjects, a courtyard can be a peaceful retreat
(PREEN MANOR, SHROPSHIRE)

The Pros and Cons

It is simple enough to define a sheltered garden. It is one that is well protected from cold winds, enjoying calm conditions. Such a garden enables one to grow a much wider range of plants than if it were open and exposed. Hopefully this book will help you to make the most of such conditions.

The book is not aimed only at gardeners living in favoured mild areas which are naturally well protected and relatively free or completely free from frost. Far from it: we look at the subject of shelter for all kinds of conditions and climates.

THE PROS AND CONS OF A SHELTERED GARDEN

A sheltered garden has many good points and can be an ideal place in which to grow plants. It may come as a surprise, therefore, to learn that even such a favourable area has a bad point or two. However, the advantages greatly outweigh the disadvantages.

Wind

Wind is one of the greatest problems as far as plants are concerned, so the more one can do to 'tame' it the better. Winds can affect many places, particularly coastal gardens and hillsides. Coastal gardens are often more windy than those inland, and there will be salt in the wind if it blows off the sea. This can severely damage non-maritime plants: it 'scorches' tender young leaves and growth. In an unprotected coastal garden it would pay to grow only true maritime plants.

Low-lying areas are generally less windy than those at higher altitude, although extensive flat areas of land which have been denuded of trees will also be very windy. Examples are heathland, moorland and grassland.

Buildings can create further wind problems, for example, in a row of detached houses with passageways or driveways between them. These gaps can form wind tunnels: the velocity of the wind is accelerated when forced through them and causes considerable damage to plants, as well as making conditions uncomfortable for people. The sheltered garden should not be troubled in this respect as steps will have been taken to filter and slow down the wind.

Another problem with wind is that it can drive rain and snow, unless the garden is sheltered. Rain which is driven hard by the wind can flatten many summer flowers. Wind-driven snow is more characteristic of higher altitudes. Wind will, of course, cause snow to pile up in drifts, leaving a lot of ground uncovered, rather than lying deeply and evenly on the ground. The latter has a lot to commend it, in fact, for a layer of snow will provide protective cover for low-growing plants during freezing conditions. This is a common occurrence in northern Europe and the northern USA, for instance, where plants are protected throughout the winter under a thick blanket of snow.

Snowfall is more gentle in sheltered gardens and forms an even blanket all over the garden. However, the disadvantage of this is that the snow will also collect on taller plants like trees and shrubs, instead of being blown away. This can cause branches to break or become distorted under the weight. The gardener has the additional chore of going round the garden gently knocking snow off branches, hedges, etc, before this can happen.

Winds can erode or blow away light soils, so this is another very good reason for providing shelter. Often, soils in coastal areas are very light and easily blown away. Winds can also cause the soil to dry out rapidly in the spring and summer, which adversely affects plants and necessitates the gardener spending more time and money on watering.

It is a well-known fact that winds can cause considerable physical damage to plants. In extreme cases plants can be blown out of the ground. More often, though, windrock is the greatest problem. As the wind whips a plant around, such as a young tree, the movement results in a hole being formed in the soil around the base of the stem. This hole inevitably becomes filled with water and in winter it may freeze. These conditions can lead to the death of the plant. Plants can be securely staked to prevent windrock; but it is much better and more convenient to have a sheltered garden.

Winds can cause other damage to plants. The leaves of evergreens can be severely scorched by cold drying winds. If young evergreen shrubs or conifers, for instance, are badly scorched they may even die. Cold drying winds in the spring can scorch young growth and buds of many other plants, too.

Winds can result in slower growth in the spring, and plants such as medium or tall hardy perennials are liable to be blown over in high summer winds. Trees can become distorted as they grow away from the wind, and lop-sided trees are a common sight in coastal areas. Climbers can be lashed around by the wind, and tree branches broken.

Soil exposed to freezing wind freezes more deeply, which is not relished by many plants. These are all very good reasons for providing shelter.

Frosts

A sheltered garden is not necessarily more protected from frost. You may not get deeply frozen soil (due to the effect of freezing winds), but late-spring frosts could damage young spring growth and flower buds, which are invariably earlier in a sheltered garden than in an exposed one. Fruit buds and blossoms are especially prone to late-spring frosts. Fruit blossoms, though, can be protected by draping the plants with fine netting at night, to keep off the frost (see Chapters 6 and 10 under Fruits, pp93 and 151).

You may wonder why late-spring frosts should be a problem in sheltered gardens. It is because the

Low-lying areas such as valley bottoms can be frost pockets because cold air drains down into them. Frost pockets can also occur on hillsides if the flow of air is impeded by a wall or dense hedge. If walls or hedges run across a slope gaps should be left in them to allow cold air through

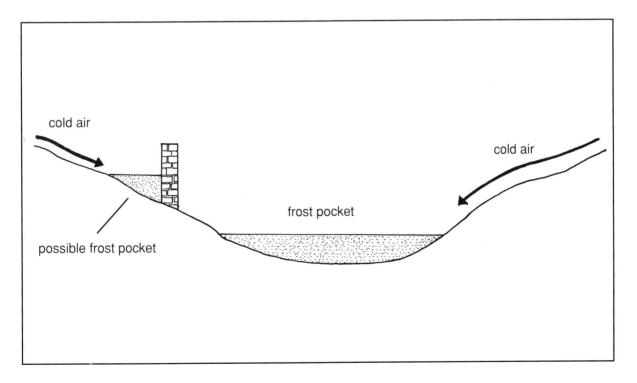

garden might be free from the effects of slight breezes, which can keep light spring frosts at bay. If you grow much fruit which flowers in the spring, it may pay to allow slight breezes through the fruit garden rather than subjecting the plants to a very still atmosphere.

Ground frosts are a problem in sheltered places, especially in low-lying areas such as valley bottoms which are frost-pockets. Cold air drains down to these low-lying places, resulting in frost. In fact, frost-pockets can also occur on hillsides if the flow of cold air is impeded, for example by a wall, fence or dense hedge. The cold air will build up against the wall or other obstruction, resulting in frost. Bear this in mind when you are erecting or planting shelter, and leave gaps in the hedges, walls, fences, etc, if they run across a slope or hillside.

Shade and Wildlife

There are other benefits from a sheltered garden, too. You should have more shady areas as a result, which will allow you to grow a wide range of plants. Many plants do not relish being in sun for all or even part of the day.

Sheltered gardens are more attractive to wildlife, such as birds and insects. Butterflies, for instance, are more likely to visit flowers in a sheltered garden than one exposed to wind. This is an important consideration these days, with conservation uppermost in the minds of many people.

SUMMARY OF ADVANTAGES

A sheltered garden:

* allows a wider range of plants to be grown.

* results in an earlier growing season. Early sowings of vegetables can be made, for instance, to ensure earlier crops.

* provides better conditions for fruit and vegetables.

* results in better growth of plants due to lack of wind.

* is free from physical damage by wind.

* does not have the problem of soil erosion.

* is not so likely to suffer from rapid drying out of soil.

* results in less work (less staking and tying of plants, for instance).

* is more likely to attract wildlife such as birds and insects.

* results in a better performance from scented plants
(the scent lingers on the air).

* ensures fewer problems from driving rain and snow.

* is less likely to suffer from deep freezing of the soil during winter.

* will have more shade, therefore providing ideal conditions for the wide range
of shade-loving plants.

* ensures more privacy due to screens, hedges, etc.

* is better for outdoor living as it is free from wind.

Shelter Through the Ages

The practice of enclosing gardens, or areas around dwellings, has been carried out for many centuries. Originally it was for the protection and shelter of people rather than plants; and this often applies today, too. Many people still like to have substantial boundary screens such as walls, fences or hedges; these are sometimes for security, but more often than not for privacy and wind protection. Such boundaries, of course, serve a dual purpose in that they also protect plants from the wind.

Even ancient civilisations, such as the Greeks, Romans and Egyptians, enclosed areas around dwellings, using walls or hedges. Roman and Greek houses featured paved courtyards, which provided cool retreats for the owners from the intense heat of the day. Such courtyards often had pools, to further help create a cool atmosphere, and were decorated with statuary and trees in pots. They were open to the sky, but surrounded on all sides by the walls of the house. Indeed, the house was built around the courtyard and all the rooms of the house led into it.

Courtyards can still be found today; indeed they are quite common in countries with warm climates, such as around the Mediterranean and in South America. For obvious reasons courtyards are not nearly so popular in countries with cool climates: here people want a sheltered but sunny area for sitting and outdoor living, and this is invariably provided by a patio. Incidentally, the correct meaning of patio is an inner courtyard, but the term is now used very loosely to mean any hard or paved area in the garden which is used for outdoor living.

In the Middle Ages, from the fifth to fifteenth century AD, dwellings were enclosed for defence. Walled castles were common, followed later by fortified manor houses (built only by the wealthy) surrounded by high walls and moats. Often within these walls gardens were created for the production of food and medicinal and culinary herbs.

Walls provided the best means of security, and their height and size were in direct relation to the lawlessness prevailing at the time. Walls were originally made from stone, and later bricks were used.

With the evolution of villages in the Middle Ages many small dwellings were surrounded by walls and fences, in order to keep out people and grazing animals. Wattle fences were often used for enclosing land (these would have made good windbreaks, too). They were followed by wooden paling fencing and, for greater security, even iron railings.

It is well-known that monasteries were surrounded by very high walls for seclusion. Less often realised is the fact that gardens were invariably cultivated within these walls, for the production of food and herbs. Often, fish were reared in ponds, as a further source of food for the monks. Self-sufficiency is not therefore a new idea – medieval monks were among the pioneers!

In the Tudor period (1485-1603) large gardens were often elaborately enclosed, with courtyards as features. These enclosures were intended to create a sense of neatness and formality. Clipped hedges were often used and have never declined in popularity. However, clipped hedges (in fact a form of topiary) have been recorded many centuries previ-

OVERLEAF
This physic garden in a well-sheltered courtyard features a wide range of medicinal plants and herbs, and is reminiscent of an old monastery garden (HERTERTON HOUSE, NORTHUMBERLAND)

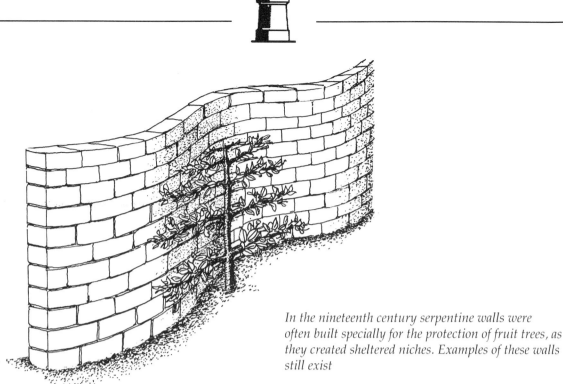

In the nineteenth century serpentine walls were often built specially for the protection of fruit trees, as they created sheltered niches. Examples of these walls still exist

ously, and the Romans practised the art of topiary.

Also in the Tudor period long wooden tunnels or arbours, which supported climbing plants, were used for both enclosing and dividing gardens.

As law and order improved, so the sizes of enclosures were reduced. Gaps were even made in them so that the surrounding countryside could be seen. Early in the eighteenth century the trend was to demolish walls enclosing estates and large gardens. A new fashion had evolved, that of making gardens blend with the surrounding countryside. This was the so-called 'landscape era', when enclosures were definitely out of fashion. However, to prevent animals from entering, gardens were surrounded by deep ditches called ha-has. Some of these still exist today around the gardens of large country houses.

The Industrial Revolution early in the nineteenth century saw the end of the 'landscape era', and started the trend towards smaller houses with enclosed gardens. Of course, there were still many large private gardens, often owned by 'captains of industry'. A common feature of these was the walled garden, an extensive area within the garden completely surrounded by high walls which created a sheltered site for the production of fruits and vegetables for the 'big house'. Invariably lean-to greenhouses were built against the sunniest walls, in which exotic fruits were grown, including pine-

apples, peaches and figs.

During the nineteenth century there was also much interest in growing trained fruits in the open. To create shelter for these walls were built within gardens, especially serpentine or crinkle-crankle walls, constructed on an undulating plan and creating sheltered niches.

Ways of enclosing gardens and providing shelter have altered little over the centuries. Nowadays we still use walls, fences, trellis and hedges, although their designs may be different. The range of materials available for walls and fences has increased, and there is a far wider choice of plants suitable for hedging. We are also more aware of the advantages of dividing gardens: this creates more shelter and shade for shade-loving plants, and provides a number of intimate 'secret areas', so creating variations in atmosphere.

Windbreaks – tall screens specifically for the purpose of slowing down the wind by filtering it, so creating very sheltered conditions on the leeward side – are a comparatively modern idea, and usually consist of lines of trees, or screens of plastic windbreak netting, etc.

GARDENING UNDER COVER

The reference to growing fruits in lean-to greenhouses brings us to another concern of this book –

gardening under cover or greenhouse gardening. This is a fascinating and complex subject from the historical point of view, which we will look at briefly here.

Throughout history the objectives of growing plants under cover have remained the same: to grow exotic plants in an otherwise unsuitable climate; to encourage more rapid growth, for example of seeds and cuttings; to manipulate the flowering and fruiting of plants; and to provide plants with weather protection (not necessarily in much higher temperatures).

Gardening under cover has been practised since Roman times, when plants were grown under thin sheets of mica, the structures probably resembling garden frames.

It was really in the late fifteenth century that quite elaborate structures first began to be constructed for the protection of plants in cool temperate climates. Then orangeries started to appear. These were merely heated shed-like structures, without natural daylight, used for protecting oranges and other citrus fruits over the winter. The trees were kept outside during warmer weather. Conservatories, as we know them today, followed on from orangeries.

It is recorded that glass was first used in orangeries during the early seventeenth century. By the end of that century orangeries were being built with bigger windows, but still had solid roofs, so did not benefit from optimum light within. From the end of the seventeenth century, however, glass was used for orangery roofs as well, as it became apparent that plants needed light in order to flourish.

In the seventeenth century the words greenhouse and conservatory came to be used, relating to structures in which plants were grown. The gardening writer John Evelyn first used the word conservatory in 1664, but also applied it to greenhouses. A conservatory was originally a structure in which tender plants were conserved in cold weather. The words conservatory and greenhouse had quite distinct meanings by the late eighteenth century. A greenhouse was used for propagating and growing plants, a conservatory for displaying and enjoying them.

From this time plant houses steadily improved; for instance, ventilation was introduced. From the early eighteenth century experiments in design increased: there was more use of lean-to structures built against walls, especially to house citrus fruits and, later, pineapples.

By early the next century many decorative tropical plants were being introduced to temperate climates by intrepid plant collectors. Large and elaborate glass structures were erected to house them.

Glass structures have long had the dual role of protecting plants and providing places for the entertainment of house guests. Since the end of the seventeenth century they have provided alternatives to summerhouses. The term 'winter garden' used to mean a massive conservatory – virtually a covered garden – which was very popular among the wealthy in the late nineteenth century. Many grand houses in Europe had winter gardens housing huge collections of the 'new' tropical plants.

Many other less wealthy, but comfortably off, people had conservatories, albeit much smaller ones, in the middle of the nineteenth century. They were similar to those of today and attached to the house with access from one of the rooms. Separate greenhouses, in which to propagate and grow plants, were also popular. Many different shapes and sizes of conservatory were built, such as dome-shaped, half-dome, curvilinear, hexagonal and octagonal. Clearer glass became available at this time, and with it a better method of bedding it (the use of putty).

Early in the twentieth century many big estates disappeared, together with the vast conservatories and winter gardens. They became too expensive to run and maintain. Gardening under cover declined with World War I, but between wars interest revived and small greenhouses became popular. After World War II some companies started to mass-produce greenhouses and conservatories, which made them more affordable. Consequently interest increased considerably. From the late 1960s and early 1970s there has been a conservatory boom, with millions being bought not only for displaying tender plants but also for providing extra living space. Today a vast range of designs is available, from traditional, such as Victorian styles, to modern.

Tremendous improvements have been made in the last few decades: we now have lightweight aluminium frameworks, double glazing for better heat retention, and complete automation of shading, ventilation, heating and watering.

Plastic now also plays a big part in undercover gardening, particularly the polythene tunnel which is so useful for vegetable production.

This cottage-style garden is in rather an open area, but is well protected by ornamental yet very functional stone walls. Note how the plants are nestling up to them – there is no doubt they are really flourishing. Prostrate conifers are growing in the path; many of these are very hardy (COATES MANOR, HAMPSHIRE)

Clipped, formal hedges have been used for many centuries for dividing gardens and providing shelter. They make an excellent background, of course, for other plants and features. These hedges enclose a formal Italian-style water garden
(COMPTON ACRES, DORSET)

Dry-stone walling can act as retaining walls as well as providing protection for plants. Although this garden is sheltered, beautiful views of the surrounding countryside have been preserved
(HIGHER LEE, LANCASHIRE)

Considering Climate

Although the sheltered garden has its own favourable climate (known as the microclimate) this does not mean to say that we can grow any plant we like outside in this type of environment. Plant choice depends particularly on the general climate, and plants should be chosen to suit this. For instance, no matter how sheltered the garden it is impossible to grow tropical plants outdoors all the year round in a cool temperate climate. Plants from cold regions might not enjoy or even survive tropical or warm-temperate climates.

GENERAL CLIMATE

The average weather conditions (sun, temperature, rain, wind, etc) of a large area or region (such as a country) constitute the general climate. This depends on many things, such as the proximity of the area or region to seas and oceans, latitude and altitude. For instance, within an extensive land mass large variations in climate are experienced, from very cold conditions in winter to tremendous heat in the summer. Alternatively, there may be extremes of wet and dry weather.

In coastal regions, however, less variation in weather conditions is usually experienced. Coastal areas often have a milder climate, and frosts may be less hard than experienced inland. Some coastal areas can be relatively frost-free, while inland frosts are a real problem for most gardeners.

In the northern hemisphere the climate is generally moister on and near western coasts and drier on and near eastern coasts. The reverse is true in the southern hemisphere. One factor which influences average temperature is altitude: the temperature decreases the higher the land is above sea level.

Warm coastal currents can influence climate. It is well-known that the climate of western Europe is tempered indirectly by the Gulf Stream, a warm current from the Gulf of Mexico which merges with the North Atlantic Drift. Winds from warmer regions passing over the North Atlantic Drift bring warmth inland, so tempering or moderating the climate of western Europe.

LOCAL CLIMATE

Local climates are the weather conditions experienced in smaller areas (for example, in parts of a country). Local climate is influenced by various factors, such as the lie of the land (slopes, hills, etc), exposure to wind and nearness to large expanses of water such as lakes.

In extensive level areas of land the climate may well be more uniform, but in mountainous or undulating areas the climate can vary over relatively small areas.

To be a good gardener it pays to get to know the local as well as the general climate really well, so that you can choose suitable plants. There may be local weather records available which would give a good indication of average climatic conditions in your area.

MICROCLIMATE

This is the climate within your garden, and even within areas of the garden. It is the only climate gardeners can modify, to some extent, to suit plants. A well-sheltered garden has a microclimate which is more favourable to plants than an exposed one. There can be several microclimates in one garden: for example, a garden could have an area of shade with moist soil, another area of shade and dry soil, a hot dry area, and so on. The more different areas the better, for then you can provide suitable conditions for a wide range of plants.

Modifying the microclimate includes providing shelter from the wind; providing shady and sunny spots; altering the soil (for instance, making it more or less moisture-retentive); providing frost protection, for instance, with greenhouses, conservatories, garden frames and cloches; providing water for plants during drought conditions; keeping excess rain off plants, for instance, by covering them with frames or cloches; and raising the temperature (again by means of greenhouses and conservatories). With a deep enough pocket to meet the fuel bills, tropical plants can be grown even in regions with long severe winters.

PLANT HARDINESS ZONE SYSTEM

Plants should always be chosen to suit the climate of the area in which the garden is located, as already discussed. Gardening books and magazines use various terms to indicate the hardiness of plants, such as 'suitable for mild areas', 'not recommended for very cold exposed areas', and so on.

The terms hardy and tender are also applied to plants. Hardy implies that a plant can survive a winter in its own climate, or another climate to which it has been introduced. Tender implies that a plant is unable to survive an average winter out-doors; this applies to introduced plants. All plants are able to survive in their own habitats.

More positive guidance is the plant hardiness zone system devised by the United States Department of Agriculture. This embraces the United States and Southern Canada.

There are 10 climatic zones, numbered from 1 to 10. Zone 1 is the coldest, and Zone 10 the warmest. An indication of the average minimum winter temperature is given for each zone.

We have attempted to apply this system also to Britain, western Europe, Australia and New Zealand.

Plants in this book have been given zone numbers where known (for example, Z8). This means that the plant should thrive in that zone, and zones with higher numbers (and therefore higher minimum winter temperatures). It is important to bear in mind, though, that there can be local variations in climate within each zone. No system dealing with plant hardiness can be completely accurate.

Warm coastal currents can influence climate. The climate of western Europe is tempered indirectly by the Gulf Stream, a warm current from the Gulf of Mexico which merges with the North Atlantic Drift

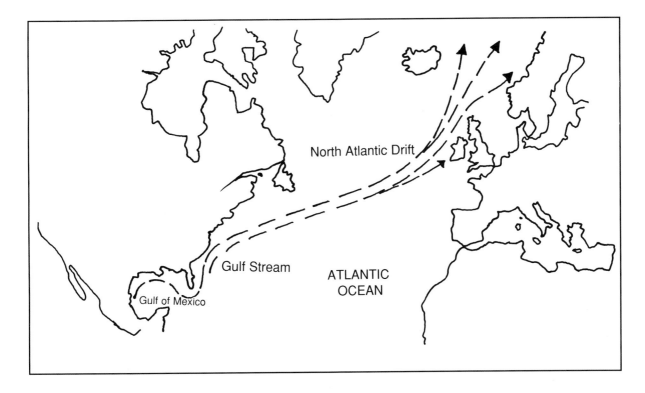

LEFT

The phormiums or New Zealand Flax have bold sword-shaped evergreen leaves. In recent years some highly colourful varieties have been introduced, which provide a tropical-looking atmosphere in sheltered, mild-area gardens (OVERBECKS, DEVON, NATIONAL TRUST)

RIGHT

Dahlias, which need to be grown in full sun, will provide a colourful summer and early autumn display in cool temperate climates, but these tender perennials are cut back by the first frosts of autumn. In regions prone to frost the dormant plants have to be overwintered indoors. Tall varieties certainly need protection from wind (UPPER WOODHILL FARM, SURREY)

BELOW

A collection of grasses and other grass-like plants, including astelia species, from New Zealand, in a mild, well-sheltered coastal garden. Southern hemisphere plants are becoming increasingly popular among gardeners in the northern hemisphere (INVEREWE GARDEN, SCOTLAND, NATIONAL TRUST FOR SCOTLAND)

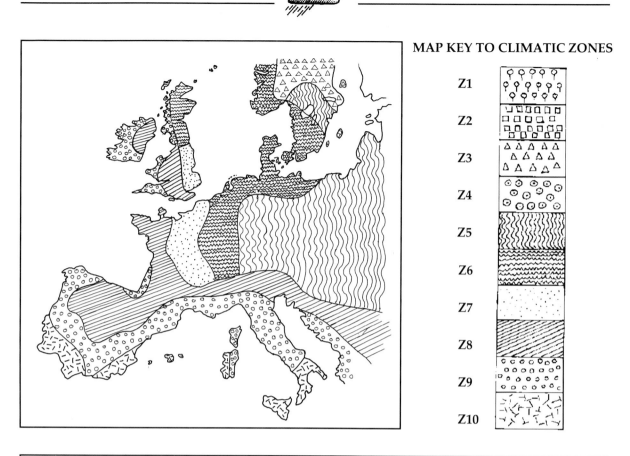

MAP KEY TO CLIMATIC ZONES

Z1
Z2
Z3
Z4
Z5
Z6
Z7
Z8
Z9
Z10

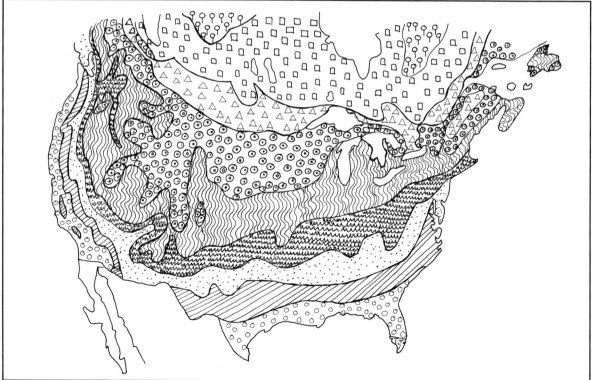

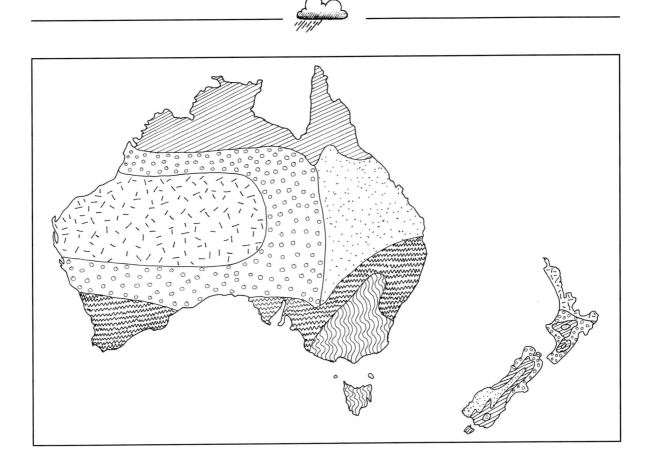

ABOVE
Climatic zones of Australia and New Zealand

ABOVE LEFT
Climatic zones of western Europe, including Great Britain. It is important to bear in mind that there can be local variations in climate within each zone

LEFT
Climatic zones of USA and Southern Canada, based on the plant hardiness zone map of the US Department of Agriculture, Agricultural Research Service

AVERAGE MINIMUM WINTER TEMPERATURES FOR THE CLIMATIC ZONES

Z1 Below −45°C (−50°F)

Z2 −45 to −39°C (−50 to −40°F)

Z3 −39 to −35°C (−40 to −30°F)

Z4 −35 to −29°C (−30 to −20°F)

Z5 −29 to −23°C (−20 to −10°F)

Z6 −23 to −18°C (−10 to 0°F)

Z7 −18 to −12°C (0 to 10°F)

Z8 −12 to −6°C (10 to 20°F)

Z9   −6 to −1°C (20 to 30°F)

Z10 −1 to   4°C (30 to 40°F)

LEFT
Many conifers, including the currently popular dwarf kinds which make such good companions for Heaths and Heathers, are very hardy, but wind protection is recommended to prevent 'scorching', particularly of young specimens (PEDLARS REST, SHROPSHIRE)

RIGHT
A typical spring bedding scheme in a cool-temperate garden. It includes hybrid bedding Tulips, Wallflowers, Pansies, and an edging of myosotis or Forget-me-not. Wallflowers will not stand up to very severe winters and are therefore best grown only in milder regions. In areas with severe winters they could be grown as pot plants in a cool greenhouse or conservatory, where they will create a fragrant atmosphere (WINKWORTH FARM, SURREY)

LEFT
Among the many hardy bulbs for cool-temperate climates are Crocuses. These are large-flowered Dutch hybrids which are popular for naturalising in grass, especially around specimen trees, where they provide welcome colour in early spring
(ROYAL HORTICULTURAL SOCIETY'S GARDEN, SURREY)

Providing Shelter

The provision of shelter from the wind should be the first consideration when taking on a garden, whether it is new or established. New gardens are usually most in need of wind protection.

The reason for urgent action is that living shelter, in the form of, say, hedges or taller windbreaks, takes time to establish. Certainly while these are settling down and gaining height temporary artificial windbreaks can be used, but they are not among the most aesthetically pleasing objects in a garden and the sooner they can be dispensed with the better.

The alternatives to hedges or taller living windbreaks are walls, fences and other permanent decorative artificial screens. These have to be chosen with care, for completely solid structures can create even more problems. Instead of filtering the wind and slowing it down, which is admirably achieved with living screens, solid structures can cause wind turbulence, which is very damaging to plants.

A combination of living and permanent artificial screens can provide suitable wind protection. The latter are relatively quick to erect and, of course, they are effective immediately they are completed, so giving you some sheltered areas long before the living screens start to do their job.

LIVING SHELTER
The advantage of living shelter, in the form of hedges or taller windbreaks, is that it filters the wind and considerably slows it down. Never try to stop the wind dead in its tracks with solid objects: this will not work as the wind will simply rush over the top of the wall for example, and plunge down violently on the other side, causing a lot of damage to plants.

The first priority should be to establish living screens on the windward boundaries of the garden. The entire garden can, of course, be enclosed if desired, which would result in an even more sheltered area.

The taller the screen, the greater the area it will protect. The sheltered zone to the leeward may extend to thirty times the height of the windbreak. However, the effect beyond twenty times the height is usually very slight. The maximum reduction of wind speed is generally at a distance of three to six times the height of the screen. For example, a 1.8m (6ft) high hedge could effectively shelter an area up to 11m (36ft) from it.

However, the height of a living screen should be in balance with the size of the garden. In today's average small garden a 1.8m (6ft) high hedge would be acceptable. Anything much taller would not only be out of proportion (and would dominate the garden), but would also create too much if not total shade and the roots would extend far into the garden.

Only large gardens, say 0.20 hectares (½ acre) and above, can accommodate tall windbreaks using lines

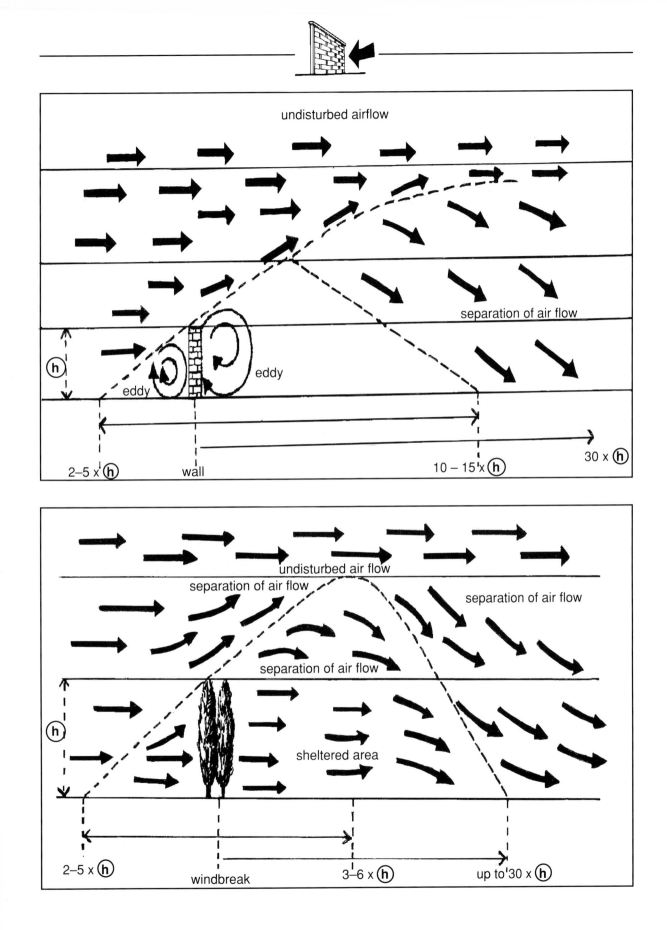

undisturbed airflow

separation of air flow

eddy

eddy

h

2–5 x h

wall

10 – 15 x h

30 x h

undisturbed air flow

separation of air flow

separation of air flow

separation of air flow

separation of air flow

h

sheltered area

2–5 x h

windbreak

3–6 x h

up to 30 x h

29

of trees which attain a height of 9-15m (30-50ft) or more. These will create sheltered conditions over a wide area: for instance, a 9m (30ft) high living windbreak could result in calm, sheltered conditions to a distance from it of about 182m (600ft) (twenty times the height). Bear in mind, too, that the spread of a tall windbreak will be much greater than, say, a hedge: think in terms of a spread of at least 3-6m (10-20ft), depending on the subject used.

Really tough subjects, which are able to stand up to cold drying winds, are commonly used for providing shelter. In mild coastal areas, though, some plants which would be damaged in colder areas inland are often able to provide good windbreaks, and withstand the salt spray well.

Hedges for protection

Hedges are often planted on boundaries in order to protect the garden from winds. However, do not make the mistake of planting a hedge too close to a boundary, otherwise it will spread on to the footpath or into the neighbour's garden. Bear in mind that the average hedge could eventually have a spread of up to 1.8m (6ft), and plant the hedge at

ABOVE
Informal hedges are ideal for informal gardens and flowering subjects are often chosen to give colour at various seasons. Many shrub roses make excellent, dense hedges and they flower in the summer. This floriferous hedge has been created with the popular hybrid musk rose 'Felicia'
(*ROYAL HORTICULTURAL SOCIETY'S GARDEN, SURREY*)

RIGHT
Beech (left), *although deciduous, makes a good dense, hedge and it holds on to its dead leaves throughout winter, when they are an attractive golden-brown shade. In front of this is a variety of Box or* Buxus sempervirens, *another popular hedging plant, this time evergreen*
(*ROYAL HORTICULTURAL SOCIETY'S GARDEN, SURREY*)

least 90cm (3ft) from the boundary.

Prepare the ground thoroughly before planting by double-digging (to two depths of the spade) a strip of ground 90-120cm (3-4ft) wide, at the same time incorporating bulky organic matter into each trench, such as well-rotted manure or garden compost. Any perennial weeds should first be killed off with a suitable weedkiller, such as one containing glyphosate.

Allow the dug strip a few months to settle before planting, then apply a general-purpose fertiliser and firm the soil well by treading.

Plant deciduous hedging subjects between late autumn and early spring if bare-rooted, or any time if containerised. Evergreens (including conifers) are best planted either in early to mid-autumn, or in mid- to late spring.

Plant them in a single line or, if you want a really wide hedge, in a double staggered row, with a distance of 38cm (15in) between the rows.

Aftercare of the newly planted hedge includes keeping the site weedfree and watering as required. A permanent mulch of bulky organic matter will help to prevent rapid moisture loss from the soil and suppress weeds. Annual feeding in the spring with a general-purpose fertiliser will ensure steady growth.

Some young hedging plants may need stout bamboo canes to support them in the early years until they are well rooted, to prevent them being loosened or blown over by strong winds. This applies especially to shallow-rooting plants like *Cupressus macrocarpa*, *crataegus* (Hawthorn) and x *Cupressocyparis leylandii*. Use your judgement: if you feel that young plants need some support, then provide it.

Likewise, some young hedging plants may need wind protection until they are well established and have toughened up. This applies especially to evergreen shrubs, including conifers, which are most vulnerable to cold drying winds in the first couple of years. A simple form of wind protection is to erect screens of windbreak netting on the windward side of the new hedge, supporting it with canes or stakes. The screen should be positioned under a metre (a couple of feet) away from the hedge and, of course, should be higher than the plants.

Young hedges need pruning to encourage dense

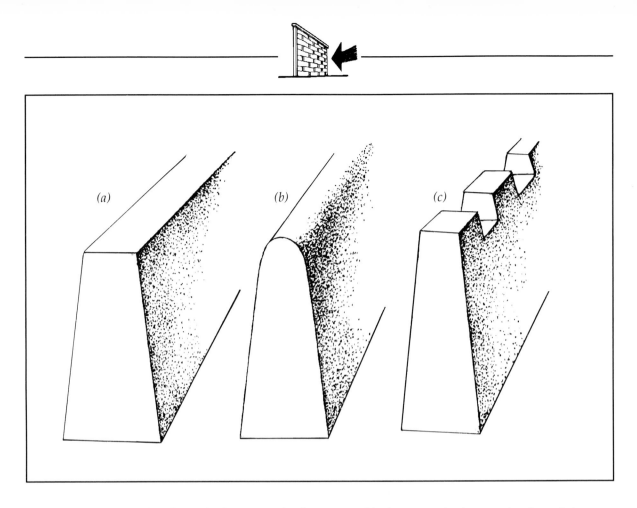

growth. With formal deciduous hedges prune back the young plants by half to two-thirds in the winter after planting. This will encourage bushy growth, especially at the base of the young hedge.

With formal coniferous hedges all you need do, if necessary, is to cut back any excessively long shoots. Conifers generally bush out quite naturally. The same comments apply to broad-leaved evergreens grown as hedges (such as ilex (Holly) and *Prunus laurocerasus).*

If you are growing an informal hedge then cut this hard back as described above for formal deciduous hedges.

In the second and subsequent years, formal deciduous hedges should be allowed to reach the required height in stages. In summer, reduce new leading shoots by half their length when they have made about 30cm (12in) of growth. Side shoots can be cut back hard in winter.

With coniferous and broad-leaved evergreen hedges, allow leading shoots to grow, but trim side shoots in late summer. Allow leading shoots to grow to 30cm (12in) above the height required, then cut them back to 15cm (6in) below this height.

Formal hedges are trained as a wedge shape, being wider at the bottom than at the top. The tops can be trained to various shapes, such as flat (a), rounded (b) or castellated (c)

After the first cutting back, allow informal hedges to grow unchecked. However, if they are not bushing out at the sides, again cut back the leading shoots by half their length in winter.

Regular trimming of hedges can be undertaken after three growing seasons. The best period to do this is between spring and early autumn

FORMAL HEDGES

These are hedges which are grown to a definite shape and need regular clipping to maintain this shape. They are very popular with owners of small gardens as they can be trained and kept quite narrow, so taking up minimum ground space. They can be deciduous or evergreen, the latter giving good shelter all the year round, unlike deciduous kinds which lose their leaves in winter.

Formal hedges can be trained as a wedge shape, wider at the bottom than at the top, with the sides sloping inwards. As a rough guide, the top of the hedge should be about half the width of the bottom, and the latter ideally should be 90-120cm (3-4ft) wide. With a wedge shape you have a stronger, denser hedge as more light is able to reach the sides, resulting in better growth. The top can be rounded or flat.

A good height for a formal hedge is 1.8m (6ft), but in a larger garden it could be allowed to grow up to 2.4m (8ft), though this is more difficult to cut.

When a formal hedge has been initially trained (see p.31) it will need to be clipped regularly but only lightly, just trimming back the new shoots. Fast-growing subjects will need to be trimmed several times during each growing season; slower-growing hedging will need to be clipped only once. For clipping times and frequencies, see the descriptive lists, pp.33-4.

The following shrubs, trees and conifers are suitable for formal hedges:

Berberis thunbergii (Barberry) (Z5) A very prickly deciduous shrub forming a dense impenetrable hedge. The variety 'Atropurpurea', with reddish-purple foliage, is recommended, and is a good choice for heavy clay or chalky soils. Plant 45cm (18in) apart; clip in mid-summer and again in mid-winter.

Buxus sempervirens (Box) (Z6) Evergreen shrub with tiny rounded dark green leaves. Excellent for chalky soils. Plant 45cm (18in) apart; trim monthly from late spring to late summer.

Carpinus betulus (Hornbeam) (Z4) Deciduous tree with large ovate green leaves. The dead foliage (golden-brown) persists throughout winter. Suitable for heavy clay or chalky soils. Plant 45cm (18in) apart; clip once, in late summer.

Chamaecyparis lawsoniana (Lawson Cypress) (Z6) An evergreen conifer with dense mid-green foliage. The best variety for hedging is 'Green Hedger'. Takes moderately exposed conditions and heavy clay soils. Plant 60cm (24in) apart; clip once in late summer.

Crataegus monogyna (Hawthorn) (Z5) Deciduous tree with lobed green leaves and very prickly shoots. Excellent for coastal gardens, very exposed situations and heavy clay soils. Plant 30cm (12in) apart; clip monthly from late spring to late summer.

x *Cupressocyparis leylandii* (Leyland Cypress) (Z5) Evergreen conifer, extremely fast-growing, with dense dark green foliage. Takes great exposure and

thrives in chalky soils; recommended for coastal gardens. Plant 60cm (24in) apart; clip once in late summer.

Cupressus macrocarpa (Monterey Cypress) (Z8) Evergreen coniferous tree with dense vivid green foliage. Not recommended for cold areas inland. Excellent for mild coastal gardens. Plant 60cm (24in) apart; clip in spring and again in late summer.

Elaeagnus x *ebbingei* (Z4) Evergreen shrub with large ovate leaves which have attractive silvery undersides. Excellent for coastal and very exposed gardens. Plant 60cm (24in) apart; clip once, in spring or late summer.

Euonymus japonicus (Z5) An evergreen shrub with ovate, shiny, deep green foliage. Tolerant of shade and pollution and highly recommended for coastal gardens. Plant 45cm (18in) apart; clip once, in spring or late summer.

Fagus sylvatica (Beech) (Z5) Deciduous tree with large mid-green ovate leaves; the dead foliage (golden-brown) persists throughout the winter. Excellent for chalky soils. Plant 45cm (18in) apart; clip once in late summer.

Griselinia littoralis (Z7) Evergreen shrub with large round leathery pale green leaves. Suitable for coastal gardens, growing well in chalky soils. Plant 60cm (24in) apart; clip once in early summer.

Ilex aquifolium (Common Holly) (Z7) Very prickly evergreen shrub with dark green foliage; or variegated in many varieties. Grows well in coastal gardens and heavy clay soils. Plant 45cm (18in) apart; clip once in late summer.

Ligustrum ovalifolium (Oval-leaved Privet) (Z6) Highly popular hedging shrub; evergreen, with small oval deep green leaves, or yellow in variety 'Aureum'. Tolerant of extreme exposure, atmospheric pollution and chalky soils. Plant 30cm (12in) apart; trim frequently between mid-spring and late summer.

Lonicera nitida (Chinese Honeysuckle) (Z7) Evergreen shrub with tiny ovate deep green leaves. Excellent for chalky and heavy clay soils. Plant 30cm (12in) apart; trim frequently between mid-spring and late summer.

Prunus cerasifera 'Nigra' (Cherry Plum, Myrobalan) (Z4) Deciduous shrub with fairly large ovate dark purple leaves. Excellent subject for chalky soils and extreme exposure. Plant 45cm (18in) apart; trim once or twice in mid-spring and early summer.

Prunus laurocerasus (Cherry Laurel) (Z7) Popular

evergreen hedging shrub with very large oval dark green glossy leaves. A good variety is 'Rotundifolia'. Do not grow in extreme exposure nor chalky soils. Plant 60cm (24in) apart; trim once in summer.

Prunus lusitanica (Portugal Laurel) (Z7) An evergreen shrub with large oval dark green shiny leaves. Excellent for extreme exposure, chalky soils and shade. Plant 60cm (24in) apart; trim once, in summer.

Pyracantha rogersiana (Firethorn) (Z6) Very spiny, dense evergreen shrub with ovate dark green foliage. Takes extreme exposure and any soil. Plant 30cm (12in) apart; trim once or twice, in spring and early summer.

Rhododendron ponticum (Common Purple Rhododendron) (Z7) Evergreen shrub with lanceolate dark green foliage. Takes extreme exposure; suitable only for acid (lime-free) soils. Plant 60cm (24in) apart; trim once in early summer.

Taxus baccata (Yew) (Z6) Evergreen conifer with dark green very narrow leaves. Quite slow growing. Tolerates extreme exposure, shade, and chalky and heavy clay soils. Plant 45cm (18in) apart; trim once in late summer.

Thuja plicata 'Atrovirens' (Western Red Cedar) (Z5) Evergreen conifer with dense vivid green shiny foliage. Excellent for chalky and heavy clay soils; not for extreme exposure. Plant 60cm (24in) apart; trim once, in late summer.

INFORMAL HEDGES

Informal hedges are allowed to grow naturally and are ideal for informal gardens if space is available for their spread. Choose shrubs which grow to around 1.8-2.4m (6-8ft) in height and bear in mind that the ultimate spread could be similar. Flowering or berrying subjects are generally chosen, to give colour at various seasons. Both evergreen and deciduous subjects can be used.

Informal hedges do not require much trimming, but if needed it is usual to do this immediately after flowering; or in spring in the case of late-summer-flowering shrubs. The only trimming that may be needed is the reduction in length of any over-long or very straggly shoots which spoil the general appearance of the hedge. On no account attempt to trim the entire hedge or you will end up with few if any flowers the following year.

The following shrubs are suitable for informal hedges:

Atriplex halimos (Tree Purslane) (Z8) Silver-grey partially evergreen foliage. Highly recommended for coastal gardens. Plant 45cm (18in) apart; trim in spring.

Berberis darwinii (Barberry) (Z6) A very prickly dense evergreen shrub with yellow flowers in spring. Excellent for chalky soils. Plant 45cm (18in) apart; trim in early summer.

Berberis x stenophylla (Barberry) (Z6) A dense prickly evergreen shrub with arching shoots carrying deep yellow flowers in spring. Excellent for chalky soils. Plant 45cm (18in) apart; trim in early summer.

Cotoneaster lacteus (Z6) Evergreen shrub with red berries in autumn, generally persisting into winter. Suitable for coastal gardens and chalky or heavy clay soils. Plant 45cm (18in) apart; trim in late summer.

Elaeagnus pungens 'Maculata' (Z7) Evergreen, with yellow-splashed foliage. Excellent for coastal gardens. Plant 60cm (24in) apart; trim in spring or late summer.

Escallonia rubra macrantha (Z8) Evergreen shrub with spikes of rose-red blooms in summer. Grows well in coastal gardens and chalky soils. Plant 60cm (24in) apart; trim in summer once flowering is over.

Forsythia x intermedia 'Spectabilis' (Z5) Deciduous shrub with bright yellow blooms in spring. Grows anywhere. Plant 45cm (18in) apart; trim in spring, when flowering is over.

Fuchsia magellanica (Z6) Deciduous shrub with deep red and violet flowers in summer. The similar *F.* 'Riccartonii' (Z6) can also be used for hedging. Suitable for coastal gardens. Plant 30cm (12in) apart; trim in early or mid-spring.

Hippophae rhamnoides (Sea Buckthorn) (Z3) Deciduous shrub with silver foliage and orange berries during autumn and winter. Suitable for coastal gardens and takes extreme exposure. Plant 60cm (24in) apart; trim in summer.

Olearia macrodonta (Daisy Bush) (Z7) Evergreen shrub with prickly leaves rather like Holly, and white daisy-like flowers in early summer. Excellent for coastal gardens and chalky soils. Won't tolerate extremely cold winds. Plant 60cm (24in) apart; trim in late spring.

Poncirus trifoliata (Japanese Bitter Orange) (Z8) Extremely spiny deciduous shrub forming an impenetrable hedge. Fragrant white blooms in spring. Plant 45-60cm (18-24in) apart; trim early summer.

Pyracantha atalantioides (Firethorn) (Z6) Evergreen

shrub with white flowers in spring and red berries
in autumn. Makes a very dense prickly hedge for
any situation. Plant 30cm (12in) apart; trim in spring
or early summer.

Rhododendron ponticum (Common Purple Rhododendron) (Z7) Evergreen shrub with lanceolate dark
green foliage. Purple flowers in early summer. Takes
extreme exposure; suitable only for acid (lime-free)
soils. Plant 60cm (24in) apart; trim in early summer
after flowering.

Rosa rugosa (Ramanas Rose) (Z2) Deciduous and
very prickly. Varieties have flowers in shades of
red, pink and white, produced during summer.
Excellent for coastal gardens. Plant 45cm (18in)
apart; trim early spring.

Symphoricarpos x chenaultii (Snowberry) (Z3) Deciduous shrub. Choose the variety 'White Hedge'.
Produces white berries in autumn. Maximum height
1.5m (5ft). Very tough and adaptable. Plant 45cm
(18in) apart; trim during summer.

Tamarix gallica (Tamarisk) (Z5) Deciduous shrub
with sprays of feathery pink blooms during summer. Excellent for coastal gardens and extreme
exposure. Not recommended for shallow chalky
soils. Plant 30cm (12in) apart; trim in early spring.

Ulex europaeus 'Plenus' (Double-flowered Gorse)
(Z7) Evergreen shrub, extremely spiny and dense,
producing its double deep yellow blooms in spring.
Grow in acid or neutral soil, including very poor
and dry soils; excellent for coastal gardens and
tolerates extreme exposure. Plant 45cm (18in) apart;
trim in spring, when flowering is over.

Viburnum tinus (Laurustinus) (Z7) Evergreen shrub
with dark green foliage and white blooms produced
in winter and spring. Suitable for coastal gardens;
grows well in chalky soils. Plant 45cm (18in) apart;
trim during spring or early summer.

Tall windbreaks

Tall windbreaks, using lines of trees which reach
heights of 9-15m (30-50ft) or more, are only recommended for large gardens. Such screens ensure that
a wide area is protected from the wind, but also cast
a lot of shade and take a great deal of moisture from
the soil during the growing season for a distance of
many metres (yards). Root spread can be great, and
this can damage foundations of buildings and
underground services like drainage systems. Therefore never plant windbreaks near to buildings.
Populus species (Poplars) have the greatest root
spread and these should be planted at least 30m
(100ft) from buildings. In fact, it is best to play safe
and allow a similar distance for other trees, too.

Deciduous and evergreen trees and conifers are
used to form tall windbreaks, and they can be mixed
if desired, to create a more attractive and pleasing
windbreak.

Plant the screen at right-angles to the direction of
the wind. The plants recommended below should
be planted in a line, 1.8-2.4m (6-8ft) apart. For a
really wide windbreak plant two parallel lines,
staggering the plants in them. Plants can always be
thinned out at a later date if necessary. Ground
preparation and planting times are the same as for
hedges.

If a tall windbreak becomes bare at the base (in other words, the trees lose their lower branches) then plant a line of tough wind-resistant shrubs in front of it. Choose from those recommended for hedges.

In the descriptive list below, heights which can be expected after a period of twenty years have been quoted. This is more sensible than trying to give ultimate heights for windbreak trees, as these can vary according to climate and soil conditions. If a windbreak becomes too tall, the trees can be lopped. However, the result of lopping is not particularly attractive as it spoils the natural habit of the trees. The following trees are suitable for tall windbreaks:

Chamaecyparis lawsoniana (Lawson Cypress) (Z6) An evergreen coniferous tree with dense mid-green foliage. Not recommended for extremely exposed positions. Good for clay soils. Height 12m (40ft) after twenty years.

x *Cupressocyparis leylandii* (Leyland Cypress) (Z5) Evergreen coniferous tree with dense, dark green leaves. Excellent for coastal gardens, extreme exposure and chalky soils. Height 15m (50ft) after twenty years.

Cupressus macrocarpa (Monterey Cypress) (Z8) Evergreen coniferous tree with dense vivid green foliage. Only recommended for milder regions; excellent for coastal areas. Height 15m (50ft) after twenty years.

Larix decidua (European Larch) (Z3) Deciduous coniferous tree with pale green leaves which turn yellow in autumn. Recommended for extremely cold or exposed areas, but not for shallow chalky soils. Height 15m (50ft) after twenty years.

Picea abies (Norway Spruce) (Z3) Evergreen coniferous tree with short vivid green needles. Grows well in chalky soils. Height 15m (50ft) after twenty years.

Pinus nigra (Austrian Pine) (Z4) Evergreen coniferous tree with dark green needle-like foliage. Suitable for extreme exposure, coastal gardens and chalky soils. Height 10m (35ft) after twenty years.

Pinus nigra maritima (Corsican Pine) (Z4) Evergreen coniferous tree with greyish-green needle-like foliage. Suitable for extreme exposure, coastal gardens and any soil. Height 12m (40ft) after twenty years.

Pinus radiata (Monterey Pine) (Z7) Evergreen coniferous tree with vivid green needle-like foliage. Only suitable for milder regions and coastal gardens. Height 15m (50ft) after twenty years.

Populus alba (White Poplar) (Z4) Deciduous tree whose leaves have white undersides. The leaves turn yellow in autumn before they fall. Excellent for wet soils and coastal gardens. Height 12m (40ft) after twenty years.

Populus canescens (Poplar) (Z4) Deciduous tree whose leaves have greyish-white undersides. The leaves turn yellow in autumn before they fall. Excellent for wet soils and coastal gardens. Height 9-15m (30-50ft) after twenty years.

Populus nigra 'Italia' (Lombardy Poplar) (Z2) Deciduous tree with light-green leaves. Very adaptable as regards soils. Narrow habit. Height 15m (50ft) after twenty years.

Populus tremula (Aspen) (Z2) Deciduous tree which is noted for its fluttering leaves – even a slight breeze will set them moving. They turn yellow in autumn before they fall. Excellent for wet soils and coastal gardens. Height 9m (30ft) after twenty years.

Quercus ilex (Holm Oak) (Z8) Evergreen tree with long dark green shiny leaves. Excellent for coastal gardens and chalky soils. Height 6m (20ft) after twenty years.

Salix alba (White Willow) (Z2) Deciduous tree with longish green leaves with silver undersides. Takes extreme exposure and is suitable for coastal gardens and very wet soils. Height 12m (40ft) after twenty years.

Sorbus aria (Whitebeam) (Z6) Deciduous tree with attractive oval leaves, which are grey-green above with white undersides. They turn yellow in autumn before they fall. Takes extreme exposure, and is suitable for coastal gardens and chalky soils. Height 6m (20ft) after twenty years.

Thuja plicata (Western Red Cedar) (Z5) Evergreen coniferous tree with dense vivid green rather shiny foliage. Not recommended for extreme exposure; best grown in moisture-retentive soil but will tolerate chalky conditions. Height 15m (50ft) after twenty years.

Tilia cordata (Small-leaved Lime) (Z4) Deciduous tree whose leaves are dark green above and lighter green below. Takes extreme exposure. Height 9m (30ft) after twenty years.

Tsuga canadensis (Eastern Hemlock) (Z3) Evergreen coniferous tree with short needle-like leaves which have conspicuous white bands on the undersides. Excellent choice for extreme exposure, and tolerant of shade. Unsuitable for shallow chalky soils. Height 9m (30ft) after twenty years.

ARTIFICIAL SHELTER

Walls and fences are often erected around the boundaries of gardens, mainly for privacy. However, solid structures will not filter and slow down the wind, but result in turbulence instead. If you are starting from scratch and want a wall or fence for wind protection as well as privacy, then opt for a semi-open (semi-permeable) type. The ideal to aim for is 40-50 per cent permeability.

Walls

Semi-openwork walls are available from many good garden centres. A typical example is screen block walling consisting of ornamental concrete blocks, each with an openwork pattern.

One can also build open-brickwork walls, using normal housebricks, as shown here. It is best to use frost-resistant bricks for garden walls.

Boundary walls are generally not more than 1.8m (6ft) high, and are often a bit lower than this. If you want greater height for wind protection it may be better to plant a hedge instead.

Walls must be built on substantial foundations, known as trench foundations. A trench is dug and is half filled with a layer of rubble or hardcore. Then follows a layer of concrete. These foundations should be wider than the wall, the width generally the same as the depth of concrete. For a wall which is to be more than six courses of bricks high you will need to dig a 50cm (20in) deep trench. The concrete mix should consist of one part cement to five parts all-in aggregate.

When building a brick wall, the bricks are laid so that they overlap, creating what is known as a staggered bond. This ensures a rigid wall. Garden walls should ideally have a damp-proof course to prevent rising damp.This is ensured by first laying two courses of low-water-absorption bricks. Your local building supplier will advise on these. Long walls need to be supported with piers or buttresses built at 3.6m (12ft) intervals.

When building a brick wall it is the usual practice to build it up at each end first. Then the centre is filled in (here bricks can be cut if necessary). The bricks are bonded with mortar which consists of one part cement to six parts soft builders' sand. Before the mortar becomes hard press the joints into a V-shape with the brick-laying trowel.

All walls should have coping bricks or blocks at the top to prevent rain from penetrating the brick-

Open-brickwork walls provide substantial screens yet are able to filter and slow down the wind. Use frost-resistant bricks for garden walls

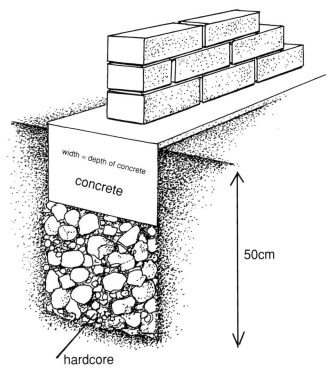

Walls must be built on substantial foundations, known as trench foundations. A trench is taken out and is half-filled with a layer of rubble or hardcore. Then follows a layer of concrete

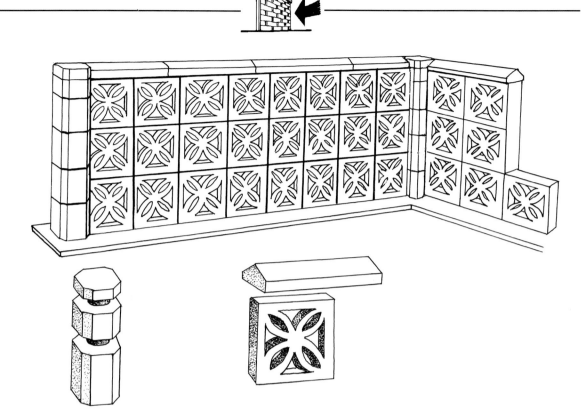

work. The coping should be laid on a damp-proof course.

Screen-block walls are built somewhat differently, the blocks being laid in stack bond, one above the other. Screen-block walls must be supported with piers built at intervals of 1.8-3m (6-10ft). The piers are built with hollow concrete cubes (known as pilasters). These have slots in them, in which the screen blocks are located. The piers themselves must be supported with vertical steel reinforcing rods. These are located through the centre of each pier and are bedded in the concrete foundations. As the piers are being built they are filled with concrete.

Special coping stones and pilaster cappings are available for use with screen-block walls.

Openwork brick walls and screen-block walls make the perfect supports for climbing plants, and plenty should be used to clothe them.

Fences and trelliswork
Semi-permeable fences should be chosen if the object is to filter the wind. They will also provide a fair degree of privacy, particularly if you go for the maximum height of 1.8m (6ft).

Ranch-type fencing is very popular for the boundaries of modern houses, and consists of wide

ABOVE
A typical semi-openwork wall is screenblock walling, consisting of ornamental concrete blocks each with an openwork pattern. Such a wall must be well supported with piers

RIGHT
*Traditionally walls were erected around the boundaries of gardens mainly for privacy. Stone was often used, as in this attractive example, though solid walls do not filter and slow down the wind, so they can result in turbulence. They do, however, make an excellent home for climbing plants, and here make a perfect backdrop for hostas and hydrangeas (*INVEREWE GARDEN, SCOTLAND, NATIONAL TRUST FOR SCOTLAND*)*

horizontal bars of timber, with spaces between them, nailed to timber posts. Generally ranch-type fencing is painted white. It makes an ideal support for climbing plants, and plenty of these should be used to further help create shelter.

Mesh fencing is widely used for boundaries, particularly on modern housing estates. There are various types available, including quite rigid plastic mesh; plastic-coated or galvanised chain-link fencing; and wire netting, which again may be galvanised or plastic-coated. Mesh fencing is often supported with steel posts, which should be galvanised and concreted into the ground. Diagonal struts are used with the end posts. Two or three heavy-duty galvanised horizontal wires are threaded through holes in the posts, and are stretched really tight by means of straining bolts located in the end posts. The mesh fencing is secured to the horizontal wires with tying wire. As mesh fencing is very open it is best to completely cover it with climbing plants to provide a greater degree of shelter.

Split chestnut palings are ideal for country gardens and consist of thin split chestnut strips linked with two or three galvanised wires. Such fencing is supplied in rolls. It is secured to stout timber posts (often chestnut poles) with galvanised-steel staples. It is very easy and quick to erect. Once again it needs to be well covered with climbing plants to afford adequate shelter.

Timber trellis panels make attractive and effective screens if clothed with climbers. They can be bought ready-made from garden centres and specialist suppliers in both traditional and modern designs with, for example, square or diamond patterns. The panels are held between stout fencing posts. The sequence of erection is to insert the first post, nail a panel to it with galvanised nails, then insert the next post and nail the other end of the panel to this.

Fencing posts must be really substantial and secure, especially in windy areas. Timber fencing posts, at least 8 x 8cm (3 x 3in) and treated with a horticultural wood preservative, can be used for most types of fencing and for trellis panels. They should be spaced 1.8m (6ft) apart and inserted 60cm (24in) into the ground. It is best to concrete them into the ground, especially if the screen will be subjected to wind buffeting. For each post dig a hole 76cm (30in) deep. Place a 15cm (6in) layer of rubble

or hardcore in the bottom and firm it well. Wedge the post upright in the centre of the hole and fill up the hole with a moderately dry concrete mix (one part cement to four parts all-in aggregate).

Steel posts for use with mesh fencing must certainly be concreted into the ground. If pointed chestnut poles are to be used for split chestnut palings, these are simply hammered into the ground to a depth of at least 60cm (24in), and preferably more on light soils.

Shelter for roof gardens and balconies
Roof gardens and balconies are often prone to wind, so they benefit from some form of protection. For a roof garden timber trellis panels could be used on the windward boundaries and clothed with climbing plants. Fixing them would have to be appropriate to the situation; it might be possible to secure them to the boundary walls. Trellis panels can sometimes be used on a balcony in the same way; perhaps at one end of a balcony, or low trellis on top of the front wall.

Temporary windbreaks
In the garden temporary windbreaks may have to be used until living screens are well established and doing their job. Indeed, hedges and taller living screens may themselves need protection in the early years until they are well established and have become tougher. Young plants are often more prone to weather damage than older ones, and this applies especially to broad-leaved evergreens and conifers. Temporary windbreaks should be erected on the windward side or sides of the garden. If used to protect young hedges or taller living screens, place them 60-90cm (2-3ft) from the hedge, etc.

Again, semi-permeable materials should be used for temporary windbreaks so that they filter and slow down the wind. The most commonly used material is plastic-mesh windbreak netting which has 48 per cent permeability. Other materials include plastic-covered fibre netting with 48-50 per cent permeability; and coir netting (or hop lewing) with 50 per cent permeability. Commercial growers often use a fairly modern windbreak material consisting of strips of plastic with gaps between, with 48 per cent permeability. This system is worth considering if you are contemplating large-scale wind protection.

Artificial windbreaks should be as tall as possible

(a)

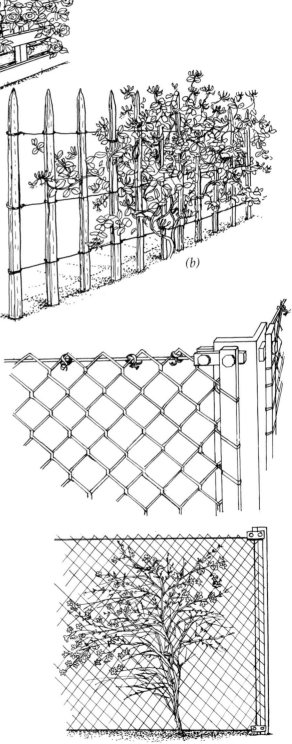

(b)

ABOVE AND RIGHT
Ranch-type fencing (a) is very popular for the boundaries of modern houses. Split chestnut palings (b) are ideal for country gardens. Both make ideal supports for climbing plants

BELOW RIGHT
Chain-link fencing is widely used for boundaries, particularly on modern housing estates, and it makes an excellent support for climbers. This combination will make a good windbreak

for maximum protection, but in the garden situation should be in scale with the garden. For instance, in the average small garden windbreaks taller than 1.8m (6ft) would look absurd. However, in large gardens windbreaks up to 3m (10ft) in height can be used. The materials recommended can be supported on a system of strained galvanised wires and substantial timber poles.

Individual plants can also be protected for the first year or two after planting with artificial screens if they are liable to weather damage. Many young broad-leaved evergreens, and conifers, for instance, are very prone to wind damage (scorching and drying of foliage) until they become established and have toughened up. Indeed, cold drying winds can kill such newly planted subjects. Protection may only be needed in the winter; but if the garden is prone to winds all the year round then leave the screens in place throughout the year. Such screens

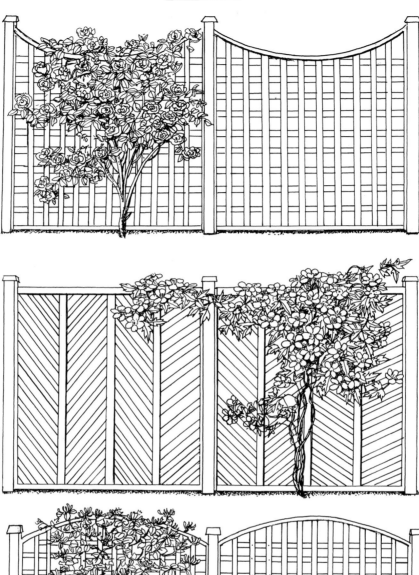

ABOVE

Timber trellis panels make attractive and effective screens, especially if clothed with climbing plants. Various modern designs are shown here and are readily available from garden centres.

RIGHT

Roof gardens are prone to be windy and therefore benefit from some form of protection. Timber trellis panels can be used on the windward boundaries, and make attractive and practical supports for climbing plants (ROOF GARDEN IN CHAPEL STREET, LONDON)

ABOVE

For the first year or two after planting individual plants can be protected with artificial screens if they are liable to wind damage. They can be surrounded with screens of windbreak netting supported with stout bamboo canes

BELOW

Wall shrubs can be protected from hard frosts with screens made from bracken, sandwiched between sheets of wire netting. These can be formed to any shape desired, although it may not always be possible to make the screen taller than the plant

are unsightly, of course, but in gardens which are not yet fully protected from wind they are essential for the establishment of vulnerable plants.

The young specimen can be surrounded with a screen of windbreak netting supported with stout bamboo canes. The screen can be in the form of a rectangle or cylinder; it must be slightly higher than the shrub or conifer, and must not be hard up against it – give the plant breathing space.

Young plants against a wall can be protected in a similar way, erecting a semi-circular screen.

PROTECTING TENDER WALL SHRUBS AND CLIMBERS

Wall shrubs and climbers which are on the border-line of hardiness (in other words, those which could succumb to a winter with hard frosts) benefit from additional protection in the winter.

One method is to weave dry bracken or straw between the stems and shoots in the autumn, and remove these materials in the spring just as growth is starting. Plenty of bracken or straw should also be placed around the base of the plant as further protection. Often if tops of stems are killed back by frost new shoots will be produced from the base of the stems in spring, provided these have been well protected.

The above system is rather messy and there is the chance that the materials will be blown away by winds or pulled out by birds. A neater method is to sandwich a layer of straw or bracken between two sheets of wire netting, which are then wired together. This 'sandwich' can then be formed to any

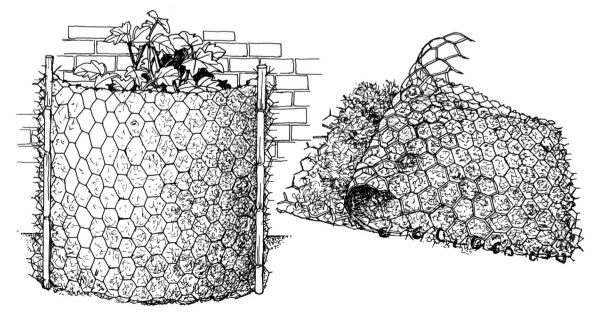

shape desired, such as a half-cylinder, then positioned in front of the wall shrub or climber. Ideally it should be taller than the plant, although this may not be possible in the case of very tall specimens, but in this instance at least part of the plant will be protected from hard frosts. This screen is easily held in place with several bamboo canes inserted into the ground around it.

Another method of protecting tender wall shrubs and climbers from excessive frost and cold drying winds is to drape several layers of windbreak netting in front of them, securing the material to the wall or fence. Do this during the severest weather in the winter. This method can also be used to protect early fruit blossoms from frost (such as wall-trained peaches and nectarines). Attach only the top of the netting to the wall or fence so that it can be lowered at night and rolled up during the day.

DIVIDING GARDENS

Dividing the garden internally so that it has a number of very secluded, sheltered and 'secret' areas is also worth considering. As well as providing additional shelter for plants, this makes any garden far more interesting than if the whole plot can be seen in one glance. Even the small pocket-handkerchief garden can be divided, if only into two areas, so do not think that only large gardens can have secluded spots.

The materials used for dividing a garden depend to a large extent on the space available. In small gardens screens need to be as narrow as possible. Trellis screens are admirable, and will not result in a claustrophobic or shut-in atmosphere. Screen-block walling would also be suitable. Climbers can be used to clothe both types of screen. In the smallest garden, the patio or other sitting area could be partially enclosed with such a screen.

In small gardens narrow formal hedges also make good screens. In larger gardens, especially if they are informal, wider informal hedges can be used. Alternatively, informal groups of large shrubs can be planted to create secluded areas.

Neither artificial nor living screens have to be in straight lines. Trellis and screen-block walling can be made into various shapes: for instance, an L-shaped screen might be appropriate. Hedges can be curved into many different shapes; in fact, straight hedges are the least imaginative in this situation. Why not consider a serpentine hedge? This is planted on an undulating plan.

Dividing a garden creates areas of shade, which is to be encouraged. A well-planned garden should have areas of shade and sun to enable a wide range of plants to be grown and to create a variation in atmosphere. A combination of cool restful shady areas and warm sunny spots makes for a more exciting and interesting garden.

When dividing a garden do not make the mistake of creating a number of boxes so that you cannot see other parts of the garden. You should also aim for some vistas or long views, each terminating in a focal point such as a statue or specimen tree or shrub, to draw the eye. Vistas give the impression of space and make the garden appear larger than it really is. The illustrations on page 48 show how to create both secluded areas and vistas.

HIDING THINGS

So far we have discussed the use of tall screens of various types to create shelter. How many of these will solve another common problem: hiding an ugly object or view? The answer is very few. In a large garden a tall windbreak consisting of a line of trees will eventually blot out everything. However, in the smaller garden the 1.8m (6ft) hedge or wall will only partially hide eyesores such as a large building or factory chimney.

In the smaller garden a small round-headed tree can be used to hide the offensive object. All too often, though, the tree is not positioned in the right place, so it fails to hide the object completely. Many people make the mistake of planting the tree near to the boundary of the garden, whereas it should be positioned further away from the object to be hidden, nearer the house or patio. This will ensure that you cannot see the object from the house or patio, although it will still be visible from beyond the tree. However, in a small garden one has to accept this. Remember that even a small ornamental tree should not be planted too close to the house for fear of roots

OVERLEAF
Dividing a garden internally with, say, hedges not only creates a number of very secluded and sheltered areas, but also makes for a more interesting garden, full of 'surprises'. A popular evergreen hedging plant has been used to divide this garden: Lonicera nitida *or Chinese Honeysuckle (EASTGROVE COTTAGE GARDEN NURSERY, HEREFORD AND WORCESTERSHIRE)*

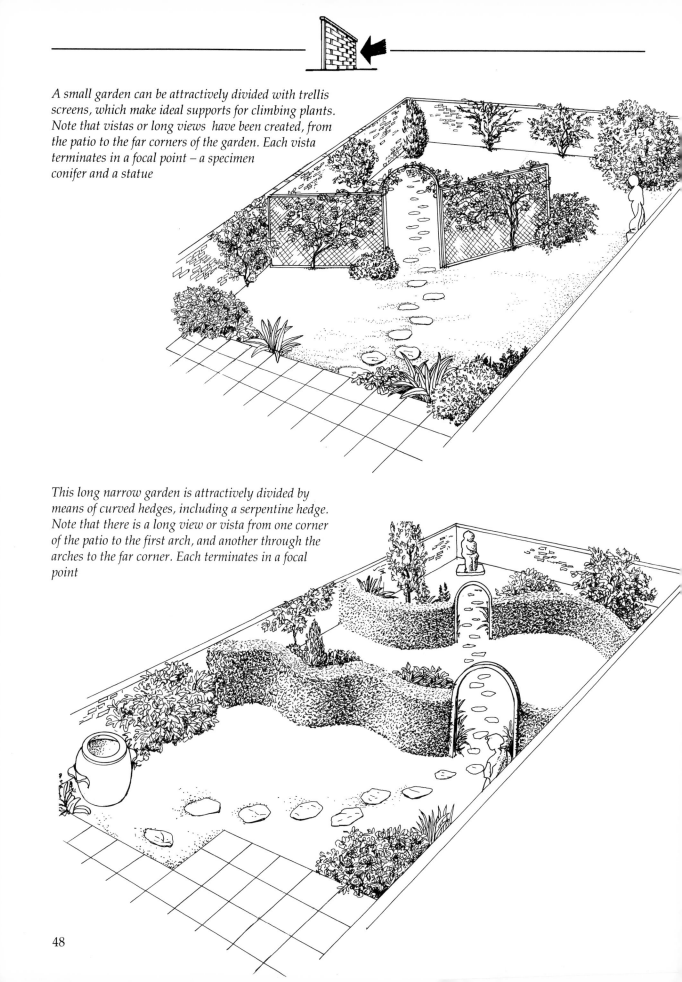

A small garden can be attractively divided with trellis screens, which make ideal supports for climbing plants. Note that vistas or long views have been created, from the patio to the far corners of the garden. Each vista terminates in a focal point – a specimen conifer and a statue

This long narrow garden is attractively divided by means of curved hedges, including a serpentine hedge. Note that there is a long view or vista from one corner of the patio to the first arch, and another through the arches to the far corner. Each terminates in a focal point

damaging foundations and drains, etc.

Suitable small round-headed trees include *Crataegus oxyacantha* varieties (Hawthorns) (Z5); Laburnums (Golden Rain Trees) (Z5); *Malus floribunda* (Ornamental Crab Apple) (Z5); *Prunus cerasifera* 'Pissardii' (Purple-leaved Plum) (Z4); Japanese Cherries (Prunus) (Z5); *Robinia pseudacacia* 'Frisia' (Z3); and *Sorbus aucuparia* varieties (Mountain Ash) (Z2). These are all deciduous and quite fast-growing.

If you want an evergreen tree then you will have to opt for a cone-shaped conifer, such as one of the taller varieties of *Chamaecyparis lawsoniana* (Lawson Cypress) (Z6). However, as these have a narrow habit and may not therefore effectively blot out a large object or view, it would be better, space permitting, to plant a group of three.

Trees in a garden have more than one role to play.

A large object can be hidden with a small round-headed tree. If sited at the far end of the garden it does not completely hide the unsightly building, but placed further away from the boundary it completely obscures it, at least when viewed from the house and patio

Apart from hiding things they also help to break the force of the wind and, very importantly, they create dappled shade, making an ideal environment for shade-loving plants. If space permits, it is highly recommended that several specimen trees are planted in a garden, choosing any of those recommended above. They can be planted in lawns or in mixed borders, ideally used as focal points to draw the eye to some particular part. Suitable positions for focal points are the end of a lawn, in a far corner, wherever a path changes direction, at the end of a path, and so on.

The technique of hiding a large object or an ugly view by positioning a tree a suitable distance from it can be used also with tall shrubs planted in groups, as well as hedges and artificial screens.

Dense boundary planting can make small gardens seem larger than they really are, for it gives the illusion of extra depth and creates the feeling that the garden extends beyond the boundaries. Furthermore, dense boundary planting creates shelter in the garden.

We are not thinking of hedges for this purpose, but wide dense plantings of tall shrubs of all kinds

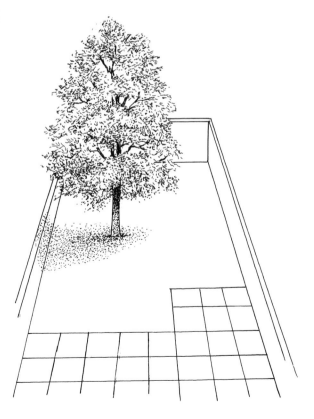

(deciduous and evergreen, flowering and foliage types). Plenty of climbing plants on the walls and fences can also make small gardens appear larger. In large towns and cities such plantings can also help to muffle noise.

When considering the question of providing shelter, hiding things and blotting out ugly views from the garden, it is worth looking at the reverse side of the coin. Some lucky gardeners have superb views from their gardens, particularly many of those living in rural or semi-rural areas. Here, one is in a dilemma. Perhaps shelter from wind is required yet at the same time one does not want to lose a particularly attractive view. Only the individual gardener can decide what to do in this situation: should the view be sacrificed in favour of a sheltered garden, or should it be completely preserved with all the consequences of high winds?

It may be possible to compromise. The most attractive part of a view could be preserved and actually 'framed' to emphasise it, say with a pair of trees or large shrubs, ideally species which are indigenous to the area. The illusion that the garden extends beyond the boundary will then be created. The rest of the boundary can then be provided with a screen for shelter. In the country it would be appropriate to plant a natural hedge. Not only would this be more in keeping than, say, a formal ornamental or flowering informal hedge of a single subject, but it would also attract a wide variety of wildlife, from birds and small mammals to insects (see Chapter 8, p.124 for further details of natural hedges).

Making the Most of Shade

Hedges, windbreaks, walls, fences, buildings and trees can all create shade. Areas of shade are a good thing in gardens for they help to create atmosphere. In shady parts of the garden the atmosphere is cool and peaceful, in contrast to the hot dry areas which are inclined to be glaring and unrestful.

Certainly shade is not the problem that many gardeners imagine, for it allows one to grow shade-loving plants to perfection. There is a wide range of suitable plants, especially among those which demand moist soil, many being choice or desirable kinds.

DRY SHADE

Shade with dry soil is one of the more challenging situations in which to grow plants, but nevertheless some attractive planting schemes can be created.

Shade with dry soil can be caused by hedges, living screens and trees. Their roots can extract large amounts of moisture from the soil, to the detriment of other plants around them.

However, roots can be cut back and kept in check to help alleviate the problem. The way to do this is to dig a 75cm (2½ft) deep trench, at least 30cm (12in) wide, cutting through the roots as you proceed. Line it to just below ground level with a sheet of thick polythene, then fill it with soil. It can be as little as 90cm (3ft) away from a hedge, or just beyond the branch spread of trees. However, there is nothing one can do about roots directly under a tree.

Large amounts of bulky organic matter dug into the soil (at least to the depth of a spade) will help to conserve moisture. Mix it into the topsoil, too. Use whatever is freely available, such as peat, pulverised bark, garden compost, well-rotted manure, leafmould, spent hops or used mushroom compost (the latter contains chalk so do not use it if lime-hating plants are to be grown).

Mulching after planting will also help to conserve moisture. This involves placing a 5-8cm (2-3in) layer of organic matter over the soil surface around the plants, and keeping it topped up regularly. Any of the materials recommended above can be used for mulching. Finally, regular and heavy watering during dry weather will help plants to establish and thrive in dry shade.

Planting schemes

All too often dry shade is an excuse for unimaginative and dull plantings. While there is only a limited number of plants that will thrive in these conditions, nevertheless some suitable combinations of these will result in colour and interest the year round.

For instance, one could form a 'framework' of evergreen shrubs like aucuba (Spotted Laurel), euonymus (Spindle), ilex (Holly) and skimmia (c). These will provide interest all the year round. Varieties of *Aucuba japonica* (Z7), like 'Crotonifolia' and 'Gold Dust', are liberally speckled with yellow; and the *Euonymus japonicus* (Z5) varieties 'Aureopictus' and 'Macrophyllus Albus' are respectively variegated with gold and white. An excellent medium-sized holly is *Ilex aquifolium* 'Ferox Argentea' (Silver Hedgehog Holly) (Z5) with very prickly cream-variegated leaves. Skimmias (Z7) will give winter interest, especially *S. japonica* 'Foremanii' which has large red berries. Plant a male skimmia with this, such as *S. j.* 'Rubella' with red winter flower buds and white blooms in spring, to ensure that berries are produced.

Drifts of perennials for spring and summer colour can be planted among these shrubs. The epidemiums (Barrenwort) (Z7) are superb for spring colour.

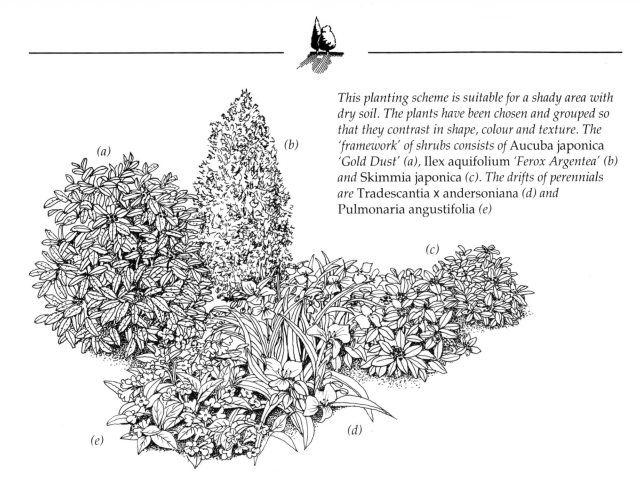

This planting scheme is suitable for a shady area with dry soil. The plants have been chosen and grouped so that they contrast in shape, colour and texture. The 'framework' of shrubs consists of Aucuba japonica *'Gold Dust' (a),* Ilex aquifolium *'Ferox Argentea' (b) and* Skimmia japonica *(c). The drifts of perennials are* Tradescantia x andersoniana *(d) and* Pulmonaria angustifolia *(e)*

The dainty young foliage of these ground-covering plants is a further attraction, often being tinted with bronze. Dainty sprays of flowers come in shades which include yellow, pink, orange and white.

Pulmonaria (Lungwort) (Z5) heralds the spring with brilliant blue flowers if *P. angustifolia* 'Azurea' is planted, or white blooms if *P. saccharata* 'Sissinghurst White' is chosen. Hardy geraniums thrive in dry shade. One of the most interesting is *G. macrorrhizum* 'Album' (Z5) with aromatic foliage and a long season of white flowers in summer. Contrasting well with this in colour and form are the varieties of *Tradescantia x andersoniana* (Spiderwort) (Z4) with their grassy foliage and incredibly long season of three-petalled flowers in shades of blue, purple or white.

It comes as a surprise to many people that the miniature hardy cyclamen (Z6)(c) thrive in dry shade. They relish these conditions, provided they are well sheltered from cold winds. The foliage is often marbled with silver, and the tiny flowers with swept-back petals come in shades of pink or white. For autumn and winter flowering try *C. coum;* for summer *C. europeum;* and for autumn *C. hederifolium (C. neapolitanum)*.

If you have some largish areas that you want to cover quickly to cut down on work, then choose the vigorous ground-cover plants *Galeobdolon luteum* 'Variegatum' (Yellow Archangel) (Z4) with evergreen silver-splashed foliage and yellow flowers in spring/early summer; any of the ivies or hederas (see Shady walls, p.7); and *Hypericum calycinum* (St John's Wort) (Z6) with large yellow flowers in summer.

MOIST SHADE
If the shady area has permanently moist soil this offers the fortunate gardener an extremely wide range of choice and desirable plants. The shade may be caused by buildings or walls; for instance, there may be a shady corner in the garden with soil which does not dry out. Quite a feature could be made of this, with a selection of flowering and foliage shrubs and perennials, and drifts of suitable bulbs. Many of these plants need shelter, which should be provided by the walls.

Most of the plants like plenty of humus in the soil, and this can be provided by digging in copious amounts of peat, leafmould or pulverised bark. These will further help to retain soil moisture.

ABOVE
Miniature hardy cyclamen will flourish in dry soil with shade, which surprises many people. This is a superb drift of Cyclamen hederifolium *(C. neapolitanum) which flowers over a long period in late summer and autumn. It is quite hardy although it originates from Greece* (COATES MANOR, WEST SUSSEX)

ABOVE LEFT
This planting scheme is suitable for a shady area with moist soil, to provide colour and interest during the winter. The 'framework' of shrubs consists of the popular Mahonia japonica *(a),* Cornus alba 'Sibirica' *(b) and* Daphne mezereum *(c). Between these drift* Helleborus orientalis *and Snowdrops* (Galanthus nivalis) *(d)*

LEFT
Summer colour and interest can be created in a shady area with moist soil by a classic combination of astilbes (a) with feathery plumes of flowers, hemerocallis or Day Lilies (b) which bloom throughout summer, and, for their bold foliage, hostas or Plantain Lilies (c). There is dramatic contrast in shape within this group

Planting schemes

Try to arrange the plants attractively, and aim to provide colour and interest all the year round. It is a good idea to provide a permanent framework of shrubs, and to drift perennials and bulbs among them.

The magnificent evergreen shrub *Mahonia japonica* (Z6)(c), with bold foliage and trusses of scented yellow flowers in winter and early spring, needs a position sheltered from cold winds. The brilliant red stems of *Cornus alba* 'Sibirica' (Z3) contrast superbly with the mahonia. Complete this winter group with *Daphne mezereum* (Mezereon) (Z5) with purplish-pink flowers in late winter.

Then drift around these shrubs *Helleborus orientalis* (Lenten Rose) (Z5)(c) with bowl-shaped flowers in shades of pink, purple, cream, etc, in late winter, not forgetting some bold clumps of Snowdrops, *Galanthus nivalis* (Z6)(c).

Herald the spring with shrubs like *Fothergilla monticola* (Z5) with its white bottle-brush-like flowers (this needs acid soil), or *Stachyurus praecox* (Z8) with catkin-like light yellow flowers. Both bloom before the leaves appear and appreciate shelter from cold winds. Drift around these shrubs small bulbs (c) like *Narcissus cyclamineus* (Z6), *N. bulbocodium* (Z6) and *Fritillaria meleagris* (Snake's Head Fritillary) (Z5), and perennials such as the ferny *Dicentra spectabilis* (Bleeding Heart) (Z3) with pink and white heart-shaped flowers.

A classic combination of perennials for summer colour consists of candelabra primulas and meconopsis (see Sheltered woodland, p.60), astilbes, ferns and hostas (Plantain Lilies).

Astilbes (Z4)(c) have feathery plumes of flowers in shades of red, pink or white, and these contrast beautifully with the other plants. Hardy ferns can include *Dryopteris filix-mas* (Male Fern) and *Matteuccia struthiopteris* (Ostrich-feather Fern).

There is a vast range of hostas (Z4)(c) available today, and collections can be seen in many gardens open to the public. They are essentially foliage plants – and bold ones at that – but they do produce spikes of lilac or white lily-like flowers in summer. Some marvellous hostas have recently been raised in America to extend the range available. Some have bluish or greyish-green foliage, such as 'Big Daddy', *H. sieboldiana* 'Bressingham Blue' and *H. s.* 'Elegans'. Others have golden foliage: 'Gold Standard', 'Golden Medallion', 'August Moon' and 'Sun Power'. Others have green and white variegated foliage: *H. ventricosa* 'Variegata', 'Thomas Hogg' and 'Francee'.

Also summer flowering are the hemerocallis hybrids (Day Lilies) (Z4)(c) with their handsome grassy foliage and long succession of lily-like flowers in many shades of yellow, orange, red, pink, etc. These look good drifted around shrubs, as does *Galtonia candicans* (Summer Hyacinth) (Z7), a bulbous plant with grassy foliage and spikes of white bell-like flowers.

An attractive autumn group could feature the evergreen shrub *Pernettya mucronata,* (Z7)(c) provided you have lime-free soil. It produces large marble-like fruits in autumn which persist well into winter. Colour depends on variety; they come in shades of pink, red and white. You must grow both male and female plants to ensure berries are produced. Around the pernettya try bold groups of *Anemone* x *hybrida* (Z5) whose varieties have pink or white flowers in autumn. Colchicums (Autumn Crocuses) complete this arrangement, such as the species *C. speciosum* with mauve flowers. The blooms appear before the leaves, which are quite large,

taking up what might be considered an unreasonable amount of space.

PEAT GARDEN

The peat garden or bed is a delightful feature for a cool shady area, such as light shade cast by walls or dappled shade from trees. It makes a home for many choice dwarf lime-hating plants, which can be grown even if your garden soil is alkaline, for the bed is raised above ground level. These plants relish a cool moist climate.

There are no rules regarding the shape or size of the bed, but it should have a minimum depth of 30cm (12in); or 45cm (18in) if the garden soil is alkaline. Compressed-peat blocks are used to build the walls of the bed and they are placed like bricks in a wall, with the joints staggered. Before use, though, soak the blocks in water for a day. When building, the joints are filled with compost (the formula is given below). It is best if the walls are angled slightly inwards as this makes them more stable. During building plant suitable plants in the joints, such as ramondas, lithospermum, haberleas and phyllodoce.

When the walls are complete place a layer of rough peat over the bottom of the bed then fill with a lime-free compost, consisting of four parts moist sphagnum peat, one part acid loam and one part coarse sand (which should be free from lime).

A layer of moist peat is placed over the compost after planting, topping it up as required. Keep the bed watered in dry periods and include the peat blocks; if these dry out they will shrink.

Choosing plants

Among the most popular plants for the peat garden are cassiopes, like *C. lycopodioides* and *C. tetragona* (Z2), diminutive evergreen shrubs with white bell-shaped blooms which herald the spring. Dwarf rhododendrons (c) are 'essential' peat-garden plants. There are many species, such as the prostrate *R. forrestii repens* (Z7) with deep red bell-like flowers, and the blue *R. impeditum* (Z6). The yellow flowers of *R. keiskei* (Z6) are a welcome sight early in the spring.

The rosette-forming ramondas, like *R. myconi* (Z7), are ideal for growing in the walls of the bed and produce blue flowers in spring. Haberleas are similar and can be grown in the same way. Well-known species include the mauve-purple *H. ferdi-*

nandi-coburgii and *H. rhodopensis* (Z6).

Hepaticas are also spring-flowering, the blooms of *H. nobilis* (Z6) coming in shades of blue, red, purple or white, depending on the form, and they may be single or double.

There are several other superb blue-flowered plants for the peat garden, including *Lithospermum diffusum* 'Heavenly Blue' (Z7) a prostrate shrubby plant which is in flower during summer and autumn and ideal for planting in the walls. *Parochetus communis* (Z9) is a somewhat clover-like prostrate perennial, except that it has brilliant blue pea-shaped flowers in summer and autumn. Then there are the autumn-flowering gentians, like *G. farreri* , *G.* x *macaulayi* and *G. sino-ornata* (Z5).

Shortias are spring-flowering evergreen perennials and the best-known species is *S. uniflora* with delightfully fringed pink blooms. A really choice plant for the peat garden is *Ourisia coccinea* (Z7), a diminutive perennial with red tubular flowers in summer and autumn. Equally worth searching for is the pink-flowered hybrid *O.* 'Loch Ewe'.

Phyllodoce aleutica (Z1) is a small evergreen shrub, rather heath-like in appearance, with small globe-shaped greenish-yellow flowers during spring and

Among the most popular plants for a peat garden are Cassiope lycopodioides *(a) with white bell-shaped flowers in spring; dwarf rhododendrons (b), either species or larger-flowered hybrids; and* Lithospermum diffusum *(c) with true blue flowers during summer and autumn*

early summer. It is ideal for planting in the peat walls.

Plants which relish a cool moist climate are the exquisite Petiolares primulas from the Himalayas, rather like *Primula vulgaris,* the primrose, in habit. Best of all is *P. whitei* with ice-blue flowers, or the variety *P. w.* 'Arduaine' with pastel-blue flowers. *P. sonchifolia* has deep china-blue flowers, while the deep pink blooms of *P. gracilipes* are set against tooth-edged leaves. All flower in the spring.

COURTYARDS
A courtyard is truly a sheltered area, being completely enclosed by high walls and usually shady. In warm climates courtyards are used as cool retreats from the sun.

The design and planting of a courtyard should be in sympathy with the cool peaceful atmosphere. In many warm countries courtyards are paved with marble, again for coolness, but this can be an expensive luxury and most people would opt for precast concrete paving slabs, perhaps in a checkerboard pattern of black and white or light and dark grey.

Traditionally the plants, mainly 'cool' foliage types, are grown in ornamental containers such as tubs or urns. Reconstituted stone containers in classical styles would be appropriate, such as imitation Greek urns. Statuary also has a place in the courtyard – perhaps imitation classical figures, again in reconstituted stone.

A formal pool in the centre of the courtyard is

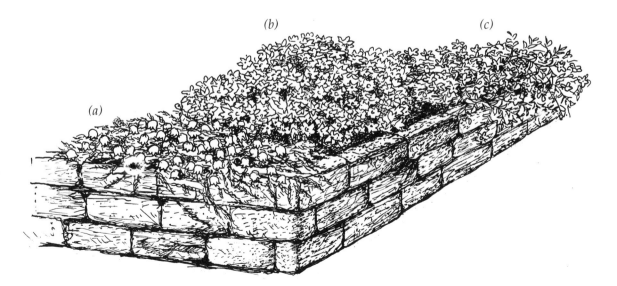

almost essential, again to help create a cool atmosphere, and if the sound of moving water can be added, so much the better as this can be very restful. Consider, for example, an ornate fountain in the centre of the pool -- perhaps one with tiered bowls in which the water trickles down from one bowl to another.

As the courtyard is the place to sit and relax, furnish it with table and chairs, such as in white-painted wrought iron. Very realistic aluminium versions are also available, and are much cheaper and lighter.

Plants with bold, flamboyant foliage are called for in the courtyard garden. The large evergreen shrub *Fatsia japonica* (Z8), with huge hand-shaped leaves and heads of white flowers in the autumn, is ideal. This can be grown in a large container, but perhaps may be better planted in a small bed in the paving. It appreciates the protection from cold winds that the courtyard garden affords.

Hostas or Plantain Lilies (Z4), as well as ferns, are perfect for courtyard gardens, and can be grown in tubs or small beds. A good selection has been described under Moist shade, p.53. Include also the

Hart's-tongue Fern, *Phyllitis scolopendrium* (Z5), with long bright green strap-shaped leaves, or the variety 'Crispum' with wavy leaves. Ferns can be tucked into any cool shady corner, perhaps grouped with the Arum Lily, *Zantedeschia aethiopica* (Z8)(c), with arrow-shaped leaves and white sail-like flowers in the summer. This plant likes moist conditions, but will not tolerate much frost. The variety 'Crowborough' is slightly tougher.

Bergenias (Z4)(c) are evergreen perennials with large, rounded, bold leaves. Their flowers in various shades of pink are borne in late winter or spring. However, for the courtyard, white-flowered bergenias are especially appropriate, like the variety 'Bressingham White'.

Rodgersias are herbaceous perennials with large bold leaves, and can be grown in tubs or beds, provided the soil is kept moist. *R. aesculifolia, R. pinnata* and *R. podophylla* (all Z4), have hand-shaped leaves. Very distinctive is *R. tabularis* (Z5) whose leaves are shaped rather like a parasol. The rodgersias produce plumes of flowers in the summer, generally pink or white, and relish protection from cold winds in a courtyard garden.

Lilies grown in tubs can be recommended for summer flowers. However, as they prefer more sun than the shady courtyard offers, they should be kept in a sunnier part of the garden until they have produced their flower buds. Then they can be transferred to the courtyard where they will bloom for many weeks. A favourite species for tub culture is the hardy *Lilium regale* (Regal Lily) with huge trumpet-shaped white scented flowers, flushed on the outside with pale purple.

All the plants mentioned so far have subtle or cool colours, but if you want some brighter splashes here and there for the summer, when the courtyard is likely to be used a great deal, consider tubs of bedding impatiens or Busy Lizzie (*Impatiens walleriana* varieties). These revel in shade and moist conditions and will be in bloom from early summer, when they are planted, until frosts start in the autumn. They are available in mixtures or separate colours, in many shades of pink, red, orange and also white if you want a cool effect. Colours are often vibrant, but recently pastel-coloured varieties have been introduced.

Mimulus hybrids enjoy the same conditions as

ABOVE RIGHT
Primulas and meconopsis or Blue Poppies are a classic plant combination for moist soil with shade. On the left is a pieris which is noted for its red young foliage. This also enjoys shade and moist soil (it must be acid)
(*SAVILL GARDENS, THE GREAT PARK, WINDSOR, BERKSHIRE*)

RIGHT
During the 'landscape era' of the eighteenth century large gardens and estates were often surrounded by ha-has rather than walls. These were deep ditches to keep out animals. This example has been attractively planted with moisture-loving plants such as astilbes and mimulus (*HIGHER LEE, LANCASHIRE*)

LEFT
The design and planting of a courtyard should be in sympathy with the cool peaceful atmosphere.
Here, plants with bold, flamboyant foliage are growing in tubs: Fatsia japonica *(a), with huge hand-shaped leaves;* Zantedeschia aethiopica *or Arum Lily (b), which sports white sail-like flowers in summer; and bergenias (c) with their large leathery leaves, which also produce red, pink or white flowers in the spring*

impatiens and produce several flushes of blooms during summer and early autumn. Like impatiens, they are also frost-tender and therefore treated as temporary plants in areas prone to frosts. Colours are vibrant – bright shades of red, yellow, orange and pink. Both impatiens and mimulus can be grown in hanging baskets if desired, which would make colourful features in the courtyard garden.

The walls of the courtyard can be clothed with climbers, choosing those which thrive in shade, such as large-leaved hederas (Ivy), x *fatshedera*, *Hydrangea petiolaris* (Climbing Hydrangea) and schizophragma (c). All of these are described under Shady walls, p.70.

SHELTERED WOODLAND

Lucky is the gardener with an area of woodland which is sheltered within from cold winds, has dappled shade and moist, humus-rich acid soil. In these conditions one can indulge in rhododendrons, especially the large-leaved kinds which need very sheltered conditions, plus other choice shrubs like pieris, many of the magnolias, camellias, kalmias and the like.

Very dense woodland, such as created by large beeches (fagus) and oaks (quercus), with very deep shade is not suitable as few plants would thrive in these conditions. The trees should cast a dappled pattern of sunlight and shade, so this may well mean thinning out the trees and maybe thinning out the canopy of each one, to create what is termed light woodland conditions. If such thinning is not possible then it may be best to leave the area to nature.

A woodland garden is quite easily created, firstly by forming meandering paths through the trees, dividing the area into large informal beds for planting. The paths can simply be formed of well-consolidated soil, but if finances permit the soil could be covered with coarse pulverised bark. Alternatively, if you can obtain some 15cm (6in) thick sections of tree trunk, these could be used as 'stepping stones' to form paths. They should be sunk into the ground so that their tops are level with the soil. It is best to first remove the bark then treat the sections with a horticultural wood preservative as this will prolong their life.

As already mentioned, the soil should be acid or lime-free, moisture-retentive and rich in humus. You can help to ensure the last two conditions by digging into the beds copious amounts of peat, leafmould or pulverised bark. Then, after planting, mulch the beds with any of these materials.

In woodland conditions the soil is at risk of drying out during dry weather in summer. This should never be allowed to happen, as many of the plants could suffer. Have some water sprinklers on standby, to which a hosepipe can be connected quickly in the event of drought conditions. If you can afford to install a permanent irrigation system, then so much the better.

Of course, not everyone has woodland, but this does not mean that you cannot grow the plants described here. If you have a very sheltered shrub border with moisture-retentive, lime-free soil, with dappled shade cast by small specimen trees, for instance, then you can certainly grow most of them. The large-leaved rhododendrons might look out of place in such a setting, but there is no reason why you should not grow many other kinds, including the small or dwarf species and hybrids.

The following plants are suitable for the woodland garden (or sheltered shrub border).

Rhododendrons

These must be the first choice for the woodland garden, and are very prominent in many large gardens open to the public. Among the most spectacular are the large-leaved species which develop into very large shrubs and tree forms, requiring a great deal of space. The following are among the best-known. *R. arboreum* (Z8) has deeply veined leaves, silvery below, and bell-shaped flowers in late winter and spring, which are deep pink in the variety 'Roseum'. The very long leaves of *R. argyrophyllum* (Z6) have white felt on the undersides and bell-shaped flowers appear in late spring, pink in the variety 'Chinese Silver'. *R. falconeri* (Z9) has deeply veined leaves and very large heads of bell-like, cream, purple-blotched flowers in mid-to late spring. The leaves of *R. fictolacteum* (Z7) are covered on the undersides with orangey-brown felt, and in mid-to late spring bell-like blooms of cream blotched with crimson are produced.

Flowering in early spring is *R. fulvum* (Z8), with shiny foliage, rust-coloured felt on the underside, and pink bell-like flowers. *R. hodgsonii* (Z8) has very long leaves with greyish felt on the undersides and, in mid-spring, bell-like purplish-pink flowers. Truly spectacular is *R. macabeanum* (Z8) with huge shiny leaves, white-felted below, and light yellow bell-like flowers in early to mid-spring.

The most famous of all large-leaved rhododendrons is *R. sinogrande* (Z8) whose leaves can be almost 1m (3ft) long. They are shiny green with silvery 'felt' below. In mid-spring massive heads of cream, crimson-blotched flowers are produced.

All these rhododendrons need to become well-established before they start flowering, and this takes many years.

There are many other rhododendron species worth growing. The following all make large specimens so require a great deal of space eventually. However, all rhododendrons are slow-growing so it will be many years before they become space-consuming. (All would adapt to container culture.)

Rhododendron augustinii (Z7) is one of the blue-flowered rhododendrons, which blooms in mid- to late spring. For a large shrub it has unusually small leaves. The peeling bark is one of the attractions of *R. barbatum* (Z8), which produces crimson bell-like flowers in large heads in early spring. It looks lovely planted with silver birches.

Rhododendron campanulatum (Z6) has attractive young foliage as it is covered with buff or brown felt. The flowers are variable in colour and may be pink or lavender-blue. As the name suggests, they are bell-shaped. With tubular orange flowers in late spring and early summer is *R. cinnabarinum* (Z8). There are several forms of this, such as *roylei* with grey-green foliage and purplish-red flowers.

Rhododendron fortunei (Z6) flowers in late spring, bearing bell-like lilac-pink blooms which are scented. *R. thomsonii* (Z8) has attractive reddish-brown bark and, in mid- to late spring, crimson bell-like flowers. A fine yellow-flowered species is *R. wardii* (Z7) which blooms in late spring.

There are literally hundreds of rhododendron hybrids, making a limited selection almost impossible to compile. The following, though, which develop into large shrubs, are bound to appeal to most gardeners.

'Christmas Cheer' (Z6) is early flowering, the blooms generally appearing in early spring. The flower buds are pink and as they open the flowers turn to white. Flowering in mid-spring is 'Cinn-keys' (Z6) with bright reddish-orange tubular flowers flushed with yellow.

One of the finest yellow hybrids is 'Crest' (Z8) with massive heads of bell-like flowers in mid-

spring. 'Cynthia' (Z6) has crimson flowers with darker markings, which are produced freely in mid-spring. Producing deep blue flowers in mid- to late spring is 'Electra' (Z8).

'Lady Chamberlain' (Z8) produces dangling, tubular flowers in mid- to late spring. There are several forms, like 'Exbury' (orange), 'Gleam' (apricot) and 'Seville' (brilliant orange).

'Loderi' (Z8) produces huge heads of flared scented flowers in early to mid-spring. There are several clones such as blush white 'King George', and pale pink 'Sir Edmund' and 'Venus'.

'Lord Swaythling' (Z8) has pink and cream flowers from reddish buds, in mid-spring, while 'Mount Everest' (Z6) bears white, brown-speckled blooms in mid-spring.

'Naomi' (Z6) is a fine hybrid. In mid- to late spring it produces pale pink flowers with a hint of yellow, which are sweetly scented. 'Shilsonii' (Z6) produces deep red bell-like blooms in early spring.

There are plenty of small rhododendrons for gardeners with limited space. It is worth obtaining *R. dauricum* (Z5) for its winter flowers which are pinkish-purple (brighter in variety 'Midwinter'). The plant makes a superb companion for hamamelis. *R. mucronulatum* (Z5) flowers at the same time and has blooms in a similar colour. *R. orbiculare* (Z6) has attractive rounded greyish-green foliage and bright pink bell-like blooms in early to mid-spring. *R. yakushimanum* (Z6) is a must for the smaller garden. Forming a compact dome of shiny green leaves, it produces white bell-like blooms from bright pink buds in late spring.

Small hybrids are numerous: particularly recommended are 'Bow Bells' (Z6) with bell-like pale pink flowers in early to mid-spring; 'Bric-a-brac' (Z8) with white blooms in early spring; 'Humming Bird' (Z8) with bright red blooms in early spring; and 'Praecox' (Z6), which blooms in late winter and early spring, the blooms being pinkish-purple.

Do not forget, either, the dwarf evergreen azaleas, particularly the Kurume hybrids (Z5) which smother themselves with flowers in various colours during late spring.

Other choice shrubs
Several other choice shrubs can be used to form the permanent framework of woodland planting schemes. Magnolias come high on the list, and collections of mature specimens can be seen in

LEFT
Woodland provides shelter in some gardens and if the soil is acid this can be a haven for rhododendrons, most of which need protection from cold winds. Notice that evergreen shrubs and conifers are also creating additional shelter (HILLIER ARBORETUM, HAMPSHIRE)

RIGHT
Hostas are extremely popular foliage plants for shade with moist soil and they associate well with many other plants which require the same conditions. Lilac or white lily-like blooms appear in summer. In the background are dwarf evergreen azaleas (SAVILL GARDENS, THE GREAT PARK, WINDSOR, BERKSHIRE)

BELOW
The peat garden is a delightful feature for a cool shady area (such as dappled shade from trees), providing a home for many choice lime hating plants. Many peat-garden plants relish a cool moist climate. This peat garden has been terraced and the beds are retained with walls made of peat blocks (ROYAL HORTICULTURAL SOCIETY'S GARDEN, SURREY)

many gardens open to the public. Some magnolias, especially the large tree types such as *M. campbellii*, *M. kobus* and *M. sargentiana*, take many years to start flowering; one may have to wait fifteen to twenty years for the first blooms to appear.

Of the large-growing tree types, *M.* 'Caerhays Belle' (Z6) is superb, with massive salmon pink flowers in late winter and early spring. *M. campbellii* (Z6) is popularly known as the Pink Tulip Tree. It has huge cup-shaped deep pink blooms in late winter and early spring. A good variety is 'Charles Raffill' with deep pinkish-purple flowers. *M. kobus* (Z6) produces its white blooms in mid-spring and is a suitable species for alkaline soils. *M. sargentiana robusta* (Z6) has massive pink blooms in early and mid-spring.

Magnolias which form large shrubs include *M.*

This classical group of hardy perennials for the woodland garden flowers in the summer. It is made up of Primula japonica *(a), one of the candelabra primulas with tiers of flowers in purplish-red;* Lilium tigrinum *(b), the reddish-orange Tiger Lily; and* Meconopsis betonicifolia *(c), the Himalayan Blue Poppy. All of these are drifted around rhododendrons*

sieboldii (Z5) which is best grown in open, sunnier woodland. The white rounded flowers, with conspicuous red stamens, hang downwards and appear between late spring and late summer. Large red fruits follow. Rather similar is *M. wilsonii* (Z6) which flowers in late spring and early summer and prefers partial shade. All of these magnolias are deciduous.

The evergreen pieris (c) are superb woodland shrubs, making medium to large specimens. They have trusses of mainly white flowers in spring. Especially good for flowers are *P. floribunda* 'Elongata' (Z5), and *P. japonica* (Z6) varieties 'Purity', 'Blush' and 'Christmas Cheer', the last two having pink-tinted blooms. Even more spectacular are the pieris with vivid red young foliage in the spring, such as *P.* 'Forest Flame', *P. formosa forrestii* and *P.f.* 'Wakehurst' (all Z6).

Hamamelis or Witch Hazels (c) are medium to large deciduous shrubs which flower in winter and look superb combined with some of the winter-flowering rhododendrons. They can be grown in slightly alkaline soils, provided these are rich in humus and moisture-retentive. The flowers consist of thin strap-shaped petals, giving a spidery appearance. A bonus comes in the form of autumn leaf tints.

Among the best hamamelis (all Z5) are varieties

(b)

(c)

(a)

of *H.* x *intermedia* like 'Allgold' (dark yellow), 'Moonlight' (light yellow), and the copper-coloured 'Diane' and 'Jelena'. There are some good varieties of *H. mollis,* too, particularly that all-time favourite, 'Pallida', with large light yellow blooms. 'Goldcrest' sports large deep yellow blooms. Also worth growing is *H. vernalis* 'Sandra' with bright acid-yellow flowers and purple-flushed young foliage, turning to brilliant flame shades in autumn.

In habit, kalmias are rather rhododendron-like, but the spring flowers, in shades of pink or red, look like blobs of icing-sugar, especially in bud. Best-known is *K. latifolia* (Calico Bush) (Z5)(c) a medium-sized shrub with pink flowers.

Also spring-flowering are the enkianthus, medium to large deciduous shrubs with clusters of bell-shaped blooms. Well-known is *E. campanulatus* (Z5) with coppery-yellow blooms.

Varieties of *Acer palmatum* (Japanese Maple) (Z5)(c) will appreciate the sheltered conditions of the woodland garden. They can be planted to form an acer glade which bursts into flame in the autumn when the leaves change colour. One of the very best varieties for autumn colour is 'Heptalobum Osakazuki', which eventually grows into a large shrub.

Camellias are essential woodland-garden shrubs, and a good selection has been recommended under Half-shade, half-sun, p.68.

Perennials and bulbs
In terms of hardy perennials, meconopsis or Blue Poppies are perfect for drifting around rhododendrons, together with candelabra primulas (described below). This theme is echoed in many gardens which are open to the public. *Meconopsis betonicifolia* (Z5) is the best-known species, but the flowers vary in colour from pure light blue to purplish. It is a short-lived perennial so new plants should be regularly raised from seeds (sown as soon as ripe). *M. grandis* (Z5) also has variable blooms of deep pure blue to purple shades. These meconopsis flower in early summer.

Candelabra primulas have their flowers arranged in whorls or tiers, these being carried on tallish stems in the summer. There are quite a few species (all Z5), such as *P. aurantiaca* (orange-yellow blooms), *P. beesiana* (pinky-purple), *P. bulleyana* (pale orange), *P. helodoxa* (deep yellow), *P. japonica* (purplish-red), and *P. pulverulenta* (deep red). Also worth growing

are one or two other primulas: *P. denticulata* (Drumstick Primrose)(c) with globular heads of pink, red, lilac, purple or white flowers in spring; *P. florindae* (Giant Cowslip), with light yellow bell-like blooms in summer; and *P. sikkimensis* (Himalayan Cowslip), bearing tubular light yellow blooms in summer.

Primulas do not mind alkaline soils provided they are moisture-retentive and rich in humus.

Trilliums are delightful spring and early summer flowering perennials with bold, three-petalled flowers. They too will succeed in alkaline soils provided these are moist and humus-rich. For impact, grow trilliums in large groups or drifts. There are several species (Z4), all low-growing plants, such as *T. erectum* (reddish-purple flowers), *T. grandiflorum* (white), *T. ovatum* (white, turning pink), and *T. undulatum* (white, zoned with purple).

There are several bulbous subjects that can be drifted among the woodland shrubs, for spring and summer colour. The first choice must be lilies which like their heads in the sun and their roots shaded by shrubs. Cool, moist, humus-rich soil is called for, and remember that some lilies will grow in alkaline soils.

The genus *Lilium* (c) is vast and there are many species and a wealth of hybrids to choose from, all flowering in the summer.

Some easy and hardy species include *Lilium davidii* with brilliant reddish-orange flowers, suitable for any soil. With light orange-yellow flowers are *L. hansonii* and *L. henryi*, the latter succeeding in alkaline soil. *L. martagon* (Turk's Cap Lily) has pinkish-purple flowers and can grow in alkaline soils.

Very striking is the pale orange, brown-spotted *L. pardalinum* (Panther Lily), which must be grown in acid soils. Also with boldly spotted flowers is the brilliant reddish-orange *L. tigrinum* (Tiger Lily) which also needs lime-free soil.

Some famous hardy hybrid lilies which are well worth growing include the mid-century hybrids such as reddish-orange 'Enchantment' and yellow 'Croesus' and 'Destiny', which are all very adaptable. Originating in America are the Bellingham hybrids, with flowers in shades of red and yellowish-orange, which are only suitable for lime-free soils. A new group of lilies known as the North hybrids have been raised at the Scottish Research Station by Dr Chris North. They have distinctive pyramid-shaped heads of flowers in a wide range of

colours, each flower carried on a long stalk. All are slightly scented, very hardy and vigorous. Look out for such names as 'Apollo', 'Theseus', 'Pandora' and 'Orestes'.

Popular trumpet hybrids include 'Black Dragon' with large white flowers, purple on the outside, and 'Golden Splendour' in deep gold. These hybrids need acid soil.

The 'king of lilies' is undoubtedly *Cardiocrinum*

giganteum (Giant Lily) which can attain a height of 3m (10ft). The stem carries huge pendulous trumpet-shaped white fragrant flowers. The Giant Lily dies after flowering, but not before producing a number of offspring, which take up to five years to reach flowering size. It needs moisture-retentive humus-rich soil and a sheltered, lightly shaded site.

Erythroniums are hardy small spring-flowering bulbs, ideal for drifting around shrubs, which often have attractive marbled foliage. The pendulous flowers have reflexed petals. The best-known species is *E. dens-canis* (Dog's Tooth Violet) with purple, pink or white flowers and bronze-marbled foliage. *E. revolutum* (American Trout Lily) has flowers in shades of pink, purple or white, which, like the foliage, are often attractively mottled. *E. tuolumnense* has yellow flowers. There is an excellent hybrid of this called 'Pagoda', also with yellow blooms, but sporting attractive coppery foliage. Shade, moisture and humus-rich soil are the ingredients for successful erythronium cultivation.

There are few more beautiful sights in the spring woodland garden than large drifts of *Anemone blanda* (Z6) with masses of starry blue flowers. There are forms with flowers in shades of pink, lilac and also white, which are suitable for any moist soil and partial shade. Do plant this anemone boldly for the best effect.

HALF-SHADE, HALF-SUN

Some plants want the best of both worlds, with some sun and some shade. For instance, lilies and clematis like their roots in cool, moist, shaded soil and their tops in the sun. (See Sheltered woodland, p.65, for details of lilies.)

Clematis (many for Z5)(c) are extremely versatile climbers for use in various parts of the garden. They are recommended for training up walls, fences and

Hydrangeas are suitable for various parts of the garden, such as the shrub border or woodland, and they flower in summer and autumn. They need shelter and protection from early morning sun. Hostas, such as H. sieboldiana 'Elegans', make admirable companions for hydrangeas , contrasting beautifully in shape and texture

pergolas, and also for growing through trees and large shrubs. The roots of clematis can be shaded by planting small shrubs around the base. Alternatively, if this is not practical or desirable, cover the root area of the clematis with some large flat pieces of stone. Clematis are ideal for alkaline soils.

Some plants need protection from early morning sun so that frozen flower buds do not thaw out rapidly, which kills them. Examples here are camellias, hydrangeas, early-flowering magnolias (see Sheltered woodland, p.64), paeonia and viburnums. Later in the day sun is acceptable, once the buds have thawed, the ideal conditions for camellias and hydrangeas being dappled shade cast by trees.

No sheltered garden with acid soil should be without camellias (c). These evergreen shrubs flower profusely in the winter or spring, and for the rest of the year their handsome glossy foliage makes an excellent background for other plants. They thrive in moisture-retentive, humus-rich soil and are obvious candidates for the woodland garden or sheltered shrub border. They relish warmth and high humidity. Areas of low rainfall are a bit more difficult for camellias, but nevertheless they can be grown provided the plants are given a very sheltered spot to protect them from cold winds..

In recent years varieties of *Camellia* x *williamsii* (Z7) have become very popular. They are derived from *C. japonica* and *C. saluenensis* and breeding was

started by J. C. Williams, of Caerhays, Cornwall (UK) in the 1930s They are the hardiest camellias available, bloom from autumn to spring, depending on variety, and have spectacularly large blooms produced in great profusion. Very hardy varieties include 'Anticipation' (pinkish-crimson double flowers), 'Bow-Bells' (pink single), 'Donation' (pink semi-double), 'Inspiration' (deep pink semi-double), 'J. C. Williams' (pink single), 'Leonard Messel' (deep pink double), and 'St Ewe' (bright pink single).

Varieties of *Camellia japonica* (Z7) are also hardy shrubs, although very hard frosts can damage flowers. Well-known varieties include 'Adolphe Audusson' (red semi-double flowers), 'Contessa Lavinia Maggi' (white and pink variegated double), 'Lady Clare' (salmon-pink semi-double), and 'Mathotiana Alba' (white double).

Varieties of *Camellia reticulata* (Z9) need sun to ripen the shoots, to ensure optimum flowering. They bloom in late winter and early spring. *C. saluenensis* (Z7), produces small flowers in shades of pink, plus white, during spring. *C. sasanqua* varieties (Z8) flower in the autumn and must be given a warm sheltered position with protection from autumn frosts. Plenty of sun is needed for optimum flowering.

A beautiful hybrid camellia is 'Cornish Snow', for which warm sheltered conditions are essential. In spring it produces a long succession of single white flowers.

Hydrangeas (c) are not recommended for very cold exposed areas, but are especially suitable for mild coastal gardens. They do need shelter and protection from early morning sun. Moisture-retentive soil is recommended, well enriched with humus. It can be acid or alkaline, but bear in mind that the blue varieties of *H. macrophylla* will only produce blue flowers on acid soils; in alkaline conditions they will be pink or purplish.

Hydrangeas are suitable for various areas such as shrub borders and the woodland garden. The hortensia and lacecap varieties of *H. macrophylla* (Z6) are superb for mass planting on a bank, provided the soil is able to retain sufficient moisture. The former group is noted for large mop-like blooms, while the latter group has flat heads of rather lacy flowers.

There are many other hydrangeas apart from *H. macrophylla*, the Common Hydrangea. For instance, try *H. quercifolia* (Z5) with deep green lobed leaves and white flowers in summer; *H. villosa* (Z7) with

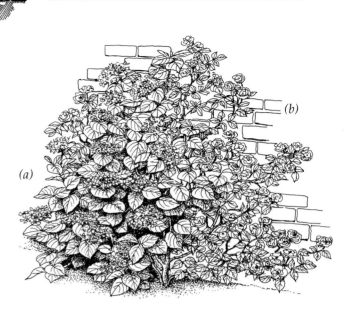

There is no shortage of climbing plants for shady walls. The climbing hydrangea, H. petiolaris *(a) is highly recommended, producing its heads of creamy-white flowers in early summer. Climbing roses (b) contrast well with this and bloom at the same time. Choose varieties which perform well on shady walls*

hairy foliage and light purple blooms in summer; and *H. aspera* (Z7) with dark green foliage, greyfelted on the undersides, and pink and blue flowers, which is unsuitable for areas which are prone to frosts in late spring.

The viburnums (c) are hardy enough shrubs and should be represented in every garden. The earlyflowering kinds, which are especially worthwhile, should be well protected from cold winds and positioned where they will not be subjected to early morning sun.

Desirable early-flowering viburnums include *V. x bodnantense* 'Dawn' (Z5), a deciduous shrub with white, pink-flushed blooms from early to late winter. *V. x burkwoodii* 'Park Farm Hybrid' (Z5) is also well worth growing. It is evergreen, bearing a profusion of white, scented flowers from pink buds from early to late spring. *V. farreri (syn. V. fragrans)* (Z6) is a popular winter-flowering deciduous shrub with fragrant white blooms, tinted with pink. *V. rhytidophyllum* (Z6) is grown as much for its superb large evergreen leaves as for its white late-spring flowers which are followed by black berries (if a group of plants is grown). The ever-popular winter-

Camellia x williamsii *'St Ewe' with* Rhododendron *'Portia' and* Betula pendula *or Silver Birch – a tasteful combination for moist lime-free soils and partial shade. Camellias should be protected from early morning sun so that frosted flower buds do not thaw out rapidly, which can kill them*
(*SAVILL GARDENS, THE GREAT PARK, WINDSOR, BERKSHIRE*)

Hydrangeas, including the lacecap types, shown here, also need protection from early morning sun so that frosted flower buds do not thaw out rapidly, which kills them. These are superb for mass planting on a bank provided the soil is able to retain sufficient moisture, for hydrangeas are very thirsty shrubs
(*OVERBECKS, DEVON, NATIONAL TRUST*)

and spring-flowering *V. tinus* 'Eve Price' (Z7) is evergreen and has flat heads of pink flowers. All of the viburnums are suitable for growing in mixed or shrub borders and succeed in any well-drained soil, being especially suitable for alkaline soils.

SHADY WALLS

Gardeners often complain about walls which receive no sun, yet there is a surprisingly wide range of climbers and wall shrubs suited to these conditions; even some climbing roses flourish and flower well on sunless walls.

If you have a peat garden (see p.56) in front of a shady wall, then an excellent wall shrub for use as a background, as it enjoys peat-garden conditions, is *Berberidopsis corallina* (Coral Plant) (Z8)(c). This is an evergreen shrub from Chile, with long deep green spiny edged leaves. In summer it produces pendulous, globe-shaped crimson flowers in clusters. Unfortunately, berberidopsis is not completely hardy and even in mild areas it should be grown in a well-sheltered position.

Wherever possible try for some attractive plant associations on the shady wall, choosing plants that contrast well in shape and colour. For instance, you could combine roses with *Hydrangea petiolaris*, schizophragma or *Jasminum officinale*. Climbing roses (Z6)(c) which perform well on shady walls include 'Aloha' (warm pink), 'Danse du Feu' (bright orange-red), 'Dortmund' (red, white centre), 'Golden Showers' (bright yellow), 'Maigold' (deep yellow), 'New Dawn' (pale pink), and 'Sympathie' (brilliant scarlet). All these are modern repeat-flowering climbers; that is, they produce a number of flushes of flowers throughout the summer and autumn.

Hydrangea petiolaris (Climbing Hydrangea) (Z5)(c) is a deciduous self-clinging climber which attaches itself to its support by means of aerial roots. It has large oval deep green leaves, a marvellous background for the creamy-white flowers which appear in early summer, when the roses also start to bloom. Like other hydrangeas, the climbing version is not recommended for very cold exposed areas.

Schizophragma hydrangeoides (Z5)(c) is a deciduous climber related to hydrangea which also supports itself by means of aerial roots. It relishes a moisture-retentive humus-rich soil. It has large attractive dark green leaves, and during mid- to late

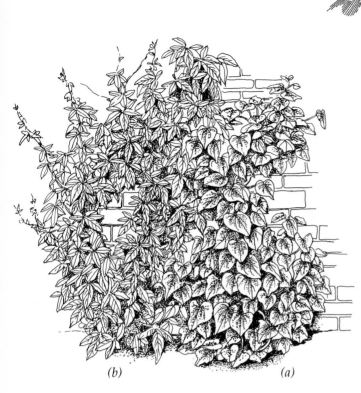

A beautiful combination of climbers for a shady wall consists of Hedera colchica *'Dentata Variegata' (a), the variegated Persian Ivy, and* Parthenocissus quinquefolia *(b), the Virginia Creeper, whose leaves take on fiery crimson tints in the autumn*

(b)   (a)

summer produces heads of small cream flowers surrounded by conspicuous light yellow bracts (modified leaves). The variety called 'Roseum' has pink-flushed bracts.

Jasminum officinale (Summer Jasmine) (Z6)(c) is a deciduous twiner and a marvellous companion for roses. It produces a profusion of scented white flowers from early summer until well into the autumn.

Another attractive combination consists of hedera (Ivy) with parthenocissus (Virginia Creeper) and cotoneaster. One has a choice of large or small-leaved ivies (c). All are evergreen, and attach themselves to their supports by means of aerial roots. Of the large-leaved ivies, *H. canariensis* 'Variegata' (Z8) is popular and highly attractive, sporting white and green variegated leaves. *H. colchica* (Persian Ivy) (Z7) also has an attractive variegated variety called 'Dentata Variegata' with cream-yellow and green foliage.

The small-leaved ivies are varieties of *H. helix* (Common Ivy) (Z5). Most popular are the variegated kinds such as 'Glacier' (grey, white and green), 'Gold Child' (edged with yellow) and 'Gold Heart' (yellow-splashed foliage). 'Buttercup' is plain yellow.

The fiery crimson autumn tints of *Parthenocissus quinquefolia* (Virginia Creeper) (Z4)(c) contrast superbly with the foliage of ivy. This is an extremely vigorous and tall-growing self-clinging climber (it attaches itself to walls by means of sucker pads), which can be kept in check by cutting it back in the summer.

The cotoneaster recommended for shady walls is *C. horizontalis* (Fishbone Cotoneaster) (Z6)(c) which can be trained perfectly flat. It is a deciduous shrub with masses of red berries in the autumn (provided the birds leave them alone), when the leaves also take on red tints. It provides a marvellous contrast to the foliage of ivies.

A superb combination for winter consists of *Garrya elliptica* (Z7)(c) and *Jasminum nudiflorum* (Winter Jasmine) (Z6)(c). The garrya is an evergreen shrub which sports greyish-green catkin-like flowers. Try to obtain the variety 'James Roof' as this has longer, more conspicuous catkins. Allow the jasmine, with its cheerful bright yellow starry flowers, to intertwine with the garrya, to give a perfect winter picture for a shady wall.

One can herald the spring with chaenomeles (Ornamental Quince) (Z5)(c) and kerria. *C. speciosa* varieties are suitable for wall training. They are deciduous shrubs with small single-rose-like flowers in shades of red, pink and white. White-flowered varieties show up especially well on a shady wall. Flowering after the Ornamental Quince is *Kerria japonica* 'Pleniflora' (Jew's Mallow, Bachelor's Buttons) (Z5), with double golden-yellow flowers. It is a deciduous shrub with erect stems – not a climbing plant as such.

The pyracanthas (Firethorns) (Z6)(c) are large evergreen shrubs which are very amenable to training on a wall. However, if you prune them too hard you will lose most of the flowers, and hence the crop of red, orange or yellow berries which is a notable feature in the autumn and winter (if the birds leave them alone). *P. coccinea* has an excellent variety called 'Lalandei' with heavy crops of large orange berries. Other good pyracanthas include 'Buttercup' with masses of small deep yellow berries; 'Golden Charmer' (orangey-yellow), 'Mohave' (brilliant reddish orange), 'Orange Charmer' (dark orange berries in profusion), 'Orange Glow' (brilliant reddish orange), and 'Watereri' (bright red berries).

An unusual climber for shady walls, and particularly recommended for courtyards, is x *Fatshedera lizei* (Z7)(c), a hybrid of *Fatsia japonica* 'Moseri' and *Hedera helix* 'Hibernica' (Irish Ivy). The large evergreen leaves are hand-shaped, dark green and glossy.

Although hardly ever produced on outdoor plants, x fatshedera has light green flowers in autumn. A variegated variety called, naturally enough, 'Variegata' has green and white leaves. Incidentally, x fatshedera is also grown as a houseplant, being ideal for a cool room.

A superb combination for winter colour on a shady wall consists of Garrya elliptica *(a), an evergreen with long greyish-green catkin-like flowers, and* Jasminum nudiflorum *(b), the Winter Jasmine, with cheerful bright yellow blooms*

(a)

(b)

Revelling in the Sun

In a garden one may well have some very hot sunny areas, perhaps with dry or extremely well-drained soil, contrasting dramatically with the shady parts. Such areas may include sunny banks, patios, south- or west-facing walls and the borders in front of them, and of course other borders and beds.

In these areas one can grow a very different range of plants to that suited to shady parts of the garden; always assuming, of course, that the garden is well-sheltered. Such areas allow one to grow many choice tender plants, including a range of Mediterranean and southern hemisphere plants, although it should be said that most of these will not be happy in areas with severe winters.

THE PROS AND CONS

The advantages of a hot and dry, or very well-drained, area have already been touched on. It allows one to grow those plants that, in the wild, thrive in such conditions. These are often very different in appearance to shade-loving plants, so you will have a garden of striking contrasts. To the sun-loving plants shade is anathema.

Very often these plants are much more drought-tolerant than shade-lovers, so you will not have to worry too much about watering during dry periods in spring and summer. However, even the sun-lovers can suffer if conditions become excessively dry, but this is really about the only problem one will have to contend with.

It is sensible to improve the soil as much as possible before planting to ensure plants do not become drastically short of moisture. Like all plants, if they are not subjected to checks to growth they will perform very much better.

Generally speaking, dry or very well-drained soils are light sandy, shallow chalky or gravelly types, containing little in the way of humus to retain moisture. Because of this the amount of humus in these soils should be increased. This is not as simple as it sounds, for humus is quickly lost in sandy, gravelly and shallow chalky soils.

In the first instance, before planting, add plenty of bulky organic matter during digging as this turns into moisture-holding humus. Use well-rotted garden compost, peat, leafmould, pulverised bark, spent hops or spent mushroom compost (not for acid soils as it contains lumps of chalk). Add a good quantity: at least a quarter of a barrowload to every 1.2m (4ft) length of trench.

Providing humus-forming materials after planting can be done by mulching the surface of the soil, again with bulky organic matter. Choose something which is also attractive in appearance, such as peat or pulverised bark. The mulching material should be spread about 8cm (3in) deep over the soil surface between and around plants. It will need topping up regularly: a peat mulch possibly annually, a bark mulch every two or three years.

Sometimes in hot dry areas gardeners use mineral mulches such as gravel (pea shingle) or stone chippings. These are often more in keeping with the area, but do not add humus to the soil. They do, however, help to prevent moisture evaporating from the soil during warm weather. Both mineral and organic mulches help to suppress the growth of annual weeds.

In light sandy, gravelly or thin chalky soils plant

A sunny corner of a courtyard makes an ideal home for many plants. This area has been tastefully planted with pale pink old-fashioned roses which harmonise beautifully with the old stone walls
(HERTERTON HOUSE, NORTHUMBERLAND)

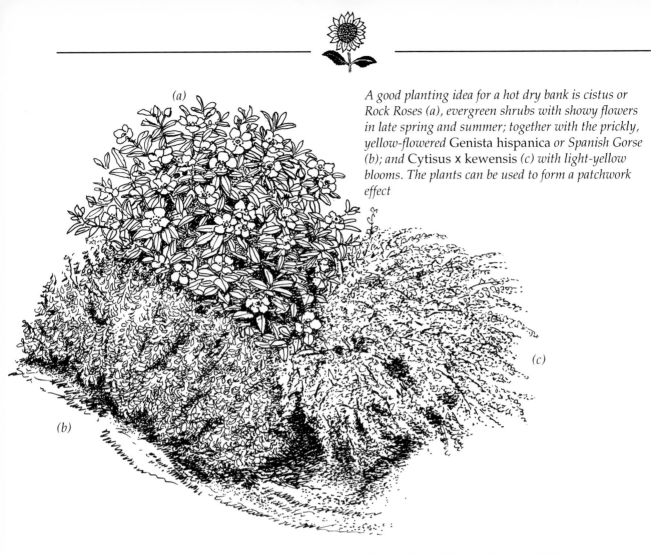

A good planting idea for a hot dry bank is cistus or Rock Roses (a), evergreen shrubs with showy flowers in late spring and summer; together with the prickly, yellow-flowered Genista hispanica *or Spanish Gorse (b); and* Cytisus x kewensis *(c) with light-yellow blooms. The plants can be used to form a patchwork effect*

foods are quickly leached out. If these are not re-placed regularly plants will suffer from nutrient deficiencies such as poor stunted growth and dis-coloured foliage. Although many of the plants rec-ommended in this chapter are accustomed to sparse conditions in the wild, we should not give them a life of poverty in the garden. They will grow and flower very much better if regularly fed. It is a good idea to use a slow-release fertiliser in these condi-tions – that is, one that releases foods slowly over a long period of time. Choose one that supplies all the major foods: nitrogen, phosphorus and potassium. Apply a base dressing before planting, pricking it into the soil surface, and then apply a topdressing annually in the spring. If, during the growing sea-son, you think that plants need a boost, they can always be given a foliar feed. This is a liquid fertil-iser which is sprayed on to the leaves of plants, where it is immediately absorbed and utilised by the plants. There are many proprietary brands of foliar fertiliser on the market.

PLANTING IDEAS FOR BANKS
A surprising number of gardeners have a steep bank to contend with. How to deal with it is proba-bly one of the most frequently-asked gardening questions. There is no lack of suitable plants for a bank, and if it is hot and dry there are some truly beautiful plants that can be grown. You could even, perhaps, create the effect of a Mediterranean hill-side.

It is recommended that a bank is planted rather than grassed. Firstly, grass is not particularly excit-ing, and therefore best reserved for the lawn. Sec-ondly, it is difficult to cut the grass on a steep bank. Really the only way you can do this is to use one of the nylon-cord trimmers.

If it is densely planted, the soil on the bank will be stabilised, preventing it from being washed down by heavy rain.

There are various ways of arranging plants on a bank. Bold groups of plants can be used to form a patchwork effect. A more unusual idea is to have wide drifts of plants meandering down the bank – rather like a river winding its way down. Some plants are better than others for this treatment: the idea works best with low or fairly low growing ground-cover type plants.

A choice of plants

The cistus (Rock Roses) (Z8)(c) are small to medium evergreen shrubs, mainly from Mediterranean areas. They are not reliably hardy in cold regions. In the late spring and summer cistus produce a succession of quite large showy flowers resembling those of single roses. The hardiest of the cistus include C. x *corbariensis* (white flowers from red buds), C. x *cyprius* (white, blotched with crimson), C. *laurifolius* (white, with yellow centre), C. x *lusitanicus* (white, blotched with crimson), C. *populifolius* (white, yellow centre) and 'Silver Pink' (light pink).

Some of the cytisus (Brooms) (Z6)(c) are excellent for covering a bank and produce masses of pea-shaped flowers in the spring. A ground-cover type hybrid is C. x *beanii* whose branches are wreathed with deep yellow flowers. Of similar habit is another hybrid, C . x *kewensis*, which completely covers itself with light yellow blooms. *C. prostratus* has a very spreading habit and quite large yellow blooms.

Related to cytisus are the genistas (also called Brooms) (Z7)(c) which flower in late spring and early summer, with yellow blooms, borne very freely. Excellent for a bank is the dwarf G. *hispanica* (Spanish Gorse), which is an extremely spiny plant with a mound- or dome-shaped habit. G. *lydia* has an arching or prostrate habit of growth. G. *pilosa* is prostrate in habit.

For another shrub with pea-like flowers do consider the double-flowered Gorse, *Ulex europaeus* 'Plenus' (Z7). The yellow blooms start to appear in early spring and continue over a long period. It is a medium-sized, very spiny shrub which looks especially attractive when combined with cistus, giving

There are two attractive, vigorous grasses suitable for large banks, where they will help to stabilise loose soil: Phalaris arundinacea *'Picta' or Reed Canary Grass (a) with green and white striped leaves; and the brilliant bluish-grey* Elymus arenarius *or Lyme Grass (b). These contrast well in shape and colour with many other plants, such as* Potentilla fruticosa *varieties (c)*

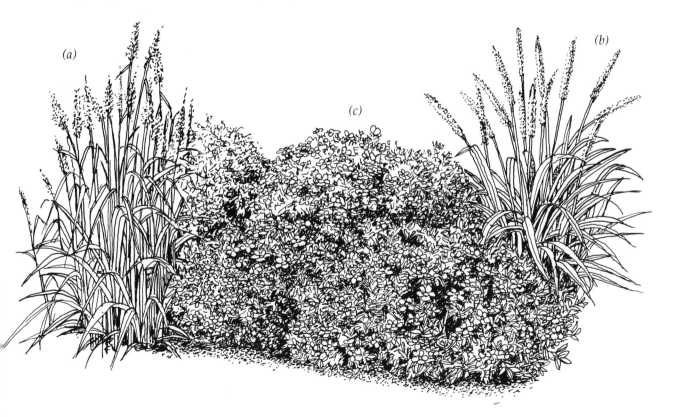

(a) *(b)* *(c)*

an excellent contrast in shape and colour.

If you have a large bank there are two very attractive ornamental grasses which are excellent for stabilising loose soil as they quickly ramify it with underground stems or rhizomes. These grasses contrast well in shape and colour with many of the other plants recommended. One is *Elymus arenarius* (Lyme Grass) (Z4), which has brilliant bluish-grey foliage. The other is *Phalaris arundinacea* 'Picta' (Reed Canary Grass or Gardener's Garters) (Z3) with white and green striped foliage, giving a very light effect overall. Both are very rampant, especially on light soils, so give them plenty of space to spread.

A group of shrubs with single rose-like flowers includes x halimiocistus, halimium, helianthemum and potentilla. x Halimiocistus (Z7)(c) is a bi-generic hybrid between halimium and cistus and forms a dwarf shrub. x *H. wintonensis* is perhaps best-known, with grey leaves and white flowers, yellow and crimson in the centre. x *H.* 'Ingwersenii' also has white flowers, and both bloom freely over a long period in summer. The halimiums are also dwarf shrubs with a somewhat spreading habit, and like x halimiocistus are evergreen. One of the most showy species is *H. ocymoides* (Z7)(c) with grey foliage which makes a marvellous background for the brilliant yellow flowers, each with a dark brown zone in the centre. They appear in the summer.

Helianthemum nummularium (Sun Rose) (Z5)(c) is a prostrate, carpeting, evergreen shrub which has a long succession of flowers in summer, in shades of yellow, orange, red, pink, etc. Named varieties are usually grown, such as 'Firedragon' (orange), 'Golden Queen' (deep yellow), 'Red Dragon' (scarlet), 'Wisley Pink' (light pink), and 'Wisley Primrose' (pale yellow).

Potentillas (Shrubby Cinquefoils) (Z6)(c) are dwarf or medium-size shrubs with a long succession of flowers during the summer. A dwarf species is *P. arbuscula* with deep yellow flowers. *P. dahurica* 'Abbotswood' is also low-growing and has white flowers set against deep green foliage. There are many varieties of *P. fruticosa*, but some good dwarf kinds suitable for banks include 'Goldfinger' (deep yellow), and 'Longacre' (brilliant yellow). Another dwarf kind is *P. parvifolia* 'Klondike' with tiny leaves and masses of deep yellow flowers.

All these plants associate particularly well with

LEFT
A sheltered sunny courtyard featuring a sub-tropical summer bedding scheme with such tender plants as eucalyptus and cordylines (PEPER HAROW, SURREY)

grey-leaved shrubs, such as Lavender (Z6)(c). Choose the dwarf Lavenders for banks, such as *Lavandula angustifolia* varieties 'Hidcote' and 'Munstead', both of which have blue flowers in summer. The Woolly Lavender, *L. lanata,* has white woolly foliage and showy violet-blue flowers. All Lavenders are evergreen.

Santolina (Cotton Lavender) are dwarf evergreen shrubs with grey or silver feathery foliage and yellow flowers in summer. The species most often grown is *S. chamaecyparissus* (Z6)(c) which has woolly silver foliage. The dwarf evergreen shrub, *Phlomis fruticosa* (Z7)(c), has greyish-green leaves and whorls of yellow flowers in late summer and autumn. Rosemary would also be suitable for drifting down a bank, provided a dwarf kind is chosen, such as *Rosmarinus lavandulaceus* (Z7)(c). This forms a carpet of evergreen foliage and produces blue flowers in spring and early summer. To succeed, it needs a really sheltered site.

BELOW
In warm sunny parts of the garden with dry, well-drained soil, one can grow a wide range of plants, as illustrated here, including silver-foliage kinds and bulbs. With the right climate and an appropriate choice of plants a Mediterranean atmosphere can be created (YORK GATE, LEEDS, WEST YORKSHIRE)

If a few larger shrubs are needed for the bank, consider Tamarisk. These deciduous shrubs have attractive feathery foliage and plumes of feathery flowers in summer. They are excellent for coastal

gardens, but unsuitable for shallow chalky soils. All Tamarisks are large shrubs and of the several species available perhaps *Tamarix parviflora* (Z5) is the most attractive, with brilliant green leaves from purplish stems and plumes of dark pink flowers in late spring and early summer.

PATIO PLANTING

The patio is probably one of the sunniest, most sheltered parts of the garden as it is used for sitting and general outdoor living. It may well be partially surrounded by walls, including the house walls, giving complete protection from cold winds. The word patio is used very loosely today to mean any paved or hard area which is used for outdoor living.

There are various ways in which a patio can be planted. It is best to opt for some particular theme, such as a Mediterranean atmosphere, which is probably more appropriate in a modern urban setting than in a country garden.

When designing a patio provide plenty of planting areas – small beds or borders around the paved area, and even little beds in the paving itself, simply achieved by leaving out paving slabs here and there. Low-growing or carpeting plants can be planted in these gaps in the paving, such as the aromatic Thymes (Z5), varieties of *Thymus serpyllum; T.* x *citriodorus;* and *T. herba-barona.* The New Zealand raoulias (Z7) are mat-forming plants and ideal for gaps in paving.

In the beds and borders around the patio include a good selection of exotic-looking plants such as the phormiums, yuccas and kniphofias. These are fully described under Gravel Areas, p.86. For summer colour, when the patio is most in use, plant temporary bedding or tender plants (c) among these, such as cannas (Indian Shot) with large bold green, bronze or purplish leaves and brilliantly coloured lily-like flowers; coleus (Flame Nettle) with multi-coloured foliage; gazanias; and dimorphothecas (African Daisies). *Ricinus communis* (Castor-oil Plant), with bold hand-shaped leaves, especially the newer bronze varieties, also gives an exotic touch.

If the patio is partially covered with a pergola, train a grape vine (c) over it to further help create a Mediterranean atmosphere. Choose the hardy *Vitis* 'Brant' (Z6) which produces black grapes, perhaps more suitable for wine-making than for dessert. In the autumn the leaves of this vine take on brilliant tints before they fall. An ornamental vine worth

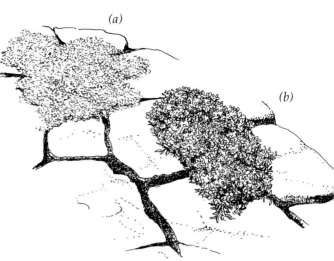

(a)

(b)

considering is *V. vinifera* 'Purpurea' (the Teinturier Grape) (Z6), with brilliant red young leaves which gradually change to dark purple as the season advances.

If you have the space against one of the walls consider planting a Fig, *Ficus carica* (Z8), with large lobed leaves and, of course, delicious fruits in the autumn. It needs a great deal of sun and very sheltered conditions. As this is such a large shrub it is a good idea to restrict the root area. Give it a narrow border, about 60cm (2ft) wide. First dig out part of the border, to a depth of 60cm (2ft) and for a length of about 1.8m (6ft). Line the sides and ends of this trough with concrete paving slabs, making sure they protrude about 2.5cm (1in) above ground level. Then place a layer of broken bricks in the bottom of the trough, about 20cm (8in) deep. Fill with good-quality loam and then plant the Fig. So contained, it will reach a height of approximately 2.4m (8ft) and will spread to at least 3.6m (12ft). Figs are also suitable for growing in tubs.

Country-garden patios need an 'English-garden' theme, with old-fashioned climbing roses (Z5)(c) in red or pink planted with large-flowered purple clematis (Z5)(c) for the pergola and walls. Introduce some old-fashioned shrub roses (Z5)(c) to the beds or borders, underplanted with Lavender (Z6)(c) or nepeta (Catmint) (Z4)(c). Herbaceous paeonias (Z3) and Flag Irises (Z5) together would provide early summer interest and contrast beautifully in shape and colour.

Suitable old-fashioned tender or bedding plants (c) for the summer include nicotiana (Ornamental Tobacco); petunias, ideally small-flowered kinds;

Low-growing or carpeting plants, such as Raoulia australis *(a) and* Thymus serpyllum *varieties (b), can be planted in gaps in paving*

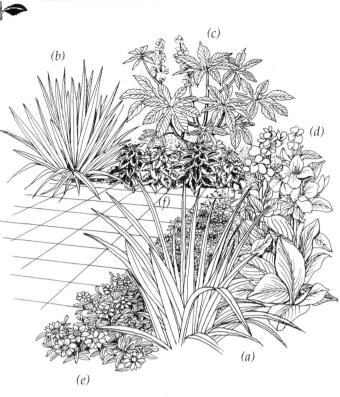

RIGHT

A patio bed or border can be permanently planted with a selection of exotic-looking plants such as phormiums (a) and yuccas (b). Among these, for summer colour, plant temporary bedding or tender plants like Ricinus communis *(the Castor-oil Plant) (c), canna or Indian Shot (d), gazanias (e) and coleus (f)*

BELOW

If a patio is partially covered with a pergola, consider training a grape vine over it to help create a Mediterranean atmosphere. The hardy Vitis 'Brant' *produces black grapes and the leaves take on brilliant tints in the autumn*

heliotrope; and nemesia. Hardy annuals (c) would be appropriate, too, like nigella (Love-in-a-mist), centaurea (Cornflower), tropaeolum (Nasturtium) and calendula (Pot Marigold).

Containers can, of course, be used on the patio, planted with suitable subjects. Use modern designs in reconstituted stone for the contemporary urban patio, and 'warm' terracotta pots or wooden half-barrels for the country patio. Any of the tender or bedding plants would be ideal for containers (see pp.80 and 81).

ROOF AND BALCONY GARDENS

Colourful gardens can be planted on flat roofs and balconies. Often these areas are very sunny, which is no problem if the right plants are chosen, although you must be prepared for rapid drying out of soil or compost. Wind could be a problem so shield the roof or balcony from its effects. Cold

RIGHT

There is certainly no lack of suitable plants for hot dry banks and one could even create the effect of a Mediterranean hillside. Dense planting helps to stabilise the soil and prevents it from being washed down by heavy rain (THE BETH CHATTO GARDENS, ESSEX)

BELOW

A country-garden patio could have an 'English-garden' theme, by planting old-fashioned flowers in the surrounding beds. A superb combination consists of tall bearded or Flag Irises (a) and herbaceous paeonias (b). Both flower in early summer, and they contrast beautifully in shape and colour

(a)

(b)

(a)

drying winds can scorch the foliage of plants, inhibit flowering and generally batter plants, causing a lot of damage.

Transparent screens are sometimes erected around the edges of roof gardens or balconies, generally on top of the walls. Plastic panels are useful, either clear or tinted if you want to preserve a view; or frosted if you wish to screen an ugly view or desire more privacy. Alternatively, timber trellis panels would make a good screen, especially if clothed with climbing plants. Choose hardy climbers (c) for this purpose – those which are able to tolerate wind, such as hederas (Z5), climbing roses (Z6), *Jasminum nudiflorum* (Z6) and *Clematis montana* (Z5).

Before starting to create a roof or balcony garden do find out how much weight it can take, whether or not you will be affecting the waterproofing system and whether excess water can drain away – you will be using a lot of water for container-grown plants. It is highly advisable to seek the advice of a structural engineer or architect, and if you are contemplating an ambitious roof garden to contact your local planning department to ensure there is no objection.

Generally plants are grown in lightweight plastic or fibreglass containers filled with lightweight soilless compost. It may also be possible to fix window boxes to the tops of balcony or roof-garden walls, but make sure they are equipped with drip trays and are securely fixed with suitable metal brackets. Hanging baskets can sometimes be hung from the ceiling of a balcony and from the house walls, using ornamental wrought-iron brackets.

A roof garden can be created with raised beds for plants provided it will take the weight. These can be built up with lightweight building blocks or timber to a height of 15cm (6in) if small plants only are to be grown, or 30cm (12in) for larger plants. Again, fill with lightweight soilless compost.

Paths between the beds, and a sitting area, could be created with lightweight aggregate, which can be obtained in several colours; alternatively use green synthetic turf.

There is no shortage of sun-loving shrubs that can be grown on roof or balcony gardens. They are all suitable for containers .Choose such kinds as lavandula (Lavender) (Z6); *Senecio* 'Sunshine' (Z8) with grey foliage and yellow flowers and the similar *S. laxifolius* (Z8); olearia species (Daisy Bushes), a number of which are described under Shrub or mixed borders(p.102); cistus (Rock Roses), described under Planting ideas for banks (p.76); *Ceratostigma willmottianum* (Z8) with blue flowers in summer and autumn; and the smaller escallonias (Z7) like 'Red Elf' with dark red flowers and the pink and white 'Apple Blossom'.

Some dwarf conifers (c) would also be suitable for the roof or balcony garden, including varieties of *Juniperus virginiana* (Z3), like 'Grey Owl' with a spreading habit and grey-blue foliage. Dwarf pines are ideal, too, provided the atmosphere is not polluted. Try *Pinus mugo* 'Gnom' or *P. m. pumilio* (Z3); and the dwarf Scot's Pine, *P. sylvestris* 'Beuvronensis' (Z3).

Raised beds on a roof garden are ideal places for many alpines or rock plants (c), particularly those kinds with a fleshy or succulent habit such as the vast range of sempervivums (Houseleeks) (Z5) and

A window box can be fitted to the top of a balcony wall with suitable metal brackets. Make sure there is a drip tray underneath it to catch surplus water. This box has been planted with continental cascade geraniums which bloom continuously throughout summer and into autumn

also the sedums (Z3). Likewise many of the sun-loving dwarf perennials should be considered, including fleshy-leaved sedums (Z3), *Centranthus ruber* (Red Valerian) (Z6) and the silver-foliage plants (see Wall borders, p.100).

On a balcony, especially, plenty of summer colour can be provided by tender bedding plants, to be enjoyed as much by passers-by as the owners. Possibly the most exciting and colourful plants to become available to more gardeners in recent years are the continental cascade or balcony geraniums, which make such a remarkable show in countries such as Switzerland and Austria. They are varieties of Ivy-leaved Geranium or pelargonium, and literally produce curtains of colour throughout summer and into autumn when grown in boxes on the edge of a balcony. They come in various shades of pink and red, and make an equally good display in hanging baskets.

All the other usual trailing summer bedding plants could be used, too, like petunias, pendulous fuchsias and begonias, and lobelia. However, do not mix them with the continental cascade geraniums as these are best grown alone. Another idea for a riot of summer colour is to grow dwarf Sweet Peas in boxes or tubs and even in hanging baskets.

Autumn on the balcony could be heralded with Charm Chrysanthemums, planted after lifting the summer bedding. You may be able to buy these, pot grown, from a local garden centre. They form neat dome-shaped mounds studded with myriad small daisy flowers in many colours. In the autumn, when the chrysanthemums have finished, plant dwarf tulips, myosotis (Forget-me-nots) and Double Daisies for spring colour.

CONTAINER CARE

All plants that are grown permanently in containers are best in soil-based potting compost. This is physically better able to support plants, especially larger kinds like shrubs, trees and climbers. Soilless or peat-based composts are fine for temporary plants like spring and summer bedding. This should be renewed annually.

Permanent plants should also have some of their compost renewed every two or three years. This can be done by removing the plant from its container, teasing away some of the compost and then placing it back in the same container, working fresh compost around the roots.

All container-grown plants benefit from regular feeding once they are established. Even temporary kinds like summer bedding plants should, once they are well-rooted into the compost, be liquid fed weekly or fortnightly. Only feed during the growing season, spring and summer. Permanent plants can be fed in the spring if desired, by applying a granular general-purpose fertiliser and pricking it into the compost surface. Then in summer give an occasional liquid feed, say every six to eight weeks.

Never allow the compost to become completely dry before watering otherwise many plants will suffer or even lose their foliage and die. Inspect containers regularly (daily or twice daily in warm conditions) and as soon as the compost is drying out on the surface give a thorough watering, so that water actually runs out of the bottom. Then you know that the entire volume of compost has been moistened. Lime-hating plants should be watered with rainwater or soft tap water (not hard or limy tap water).

As far as permanent plants are concerned, it is not generally a good idea to put a small plant into a large container for it will have too great a volume of compost around its roots, which can then remain saturated with water and lead to root rot. Practise the technique of potting on, which involves starting off a plant in a small container and gradually moving it on until it is in a large final size. The best time for potting on is early spring.

When considering the winter protection of plants in containers, remember that if the compost remains frozen solid for a prolonged spell it can result in the death of the plants (even though they are hardy kinds) for they will not be able to absorb moisture and also the roots may be killed. So in areas which are subjected to hard frosts in winter (Zone 9 and below) it pays to insulate the containers for the winter by wrapping them with a thick layer of straw or bracken, which can be held in place with wire netting.

Another way of protecting plants in containers is to move them into a frost-free but cool greenhouse for the winter, especially those which are particularly sensitive, like agapanthus (African Lilies), hardy fuchsias and camellias. Indeed, this is a sensible step to take in areas subjected to severe winters. For instance, most evergreen shrubs would not tolerate hard winters outdoors in containers, and neither would spring bedding plants.

If you live in a cold climate and do not relish the thought of moving containers under glass for the winter, then obviously you should consider growing only temporary plants for summer display, and leave the containers empty over winter.

At the other extreme, there can be problems with container plants in warm or hot climates. Here the compost can become too hot for the plants. In this instance one must aim to shade the containers, but ensure the plants receive plenty of sun (provided they are sun-lovers, of course). One way is to grow plenty of trailing foliage plants so that the containers are virtually hidden. Containers can also be clustered together so that they shade each other. A further bonus is that if they are to be hidden in this way, one can opt for relatively cheap utility kinds, rather than expensive ornate ones.

GRAVEL AREAS

A gravel area planted with a collection of bold dramatic plants is an unusual but very attractive idea for a modern, perhaps formal, garden. If you have a sunny, very well-drained corner this would be ideal for a gravel feature.

What is the purpose of the gravel? Why not simply leave the soil exposed? Well, gravel creates a variation in textures, contrasting beautifully with paving and lawn. It makes a marvellous background for plants, which really show up well against this somewhat neutral material. Furthermore, gravel makes for a labour-saving area as it suppresses the growth of annual weeds.

Firstly, the plants should be planted, grouping them so that they they contrast well in shape, colour and texture. If you wish to walk between the plants then paths should be formed simply by firming the soil really well. Finally, the soil over the entire area (including the firmed paths) is covered with a layer of gravel. The most freely available form is pea shingle, supplied by builders' merchants. Spread it at least 2.5cm (1in) thick, but no more than 5cm (2in).

A choice of plants

The phormiums (New Zealand Flax) (Z7)(c) have bold sword-shaped evergreen leaves. In recent years some highly colourful varieties have been introduced, looking almost like tropical cordylines and dracaenas. However, a very hard winter could kill

these plants.

The tallest phormiums, up to 3m (10ft) in height, are *P. tenax* and its varieties. The species has plain green leaves, but the variety 'Purpureum' has purple foliage and 'Variegatum' is striped with cream and green. Shorter kinds include *P. cookianum* 'Cream Delight' with cream leaves edged with green. Smaller *P. tenax* varieties include 'Maori Sunrise' in pink, bronze and orange; 'Sundowner' (purple and pink), 'Yellow Wave' (striped deep yellow and green), 'Dazzler' (purple and red), 'Sunset' (apricot and bronze), and 'Tricolor' (cream, silver and green). New varieties being introduced all the time seem to be more and more colourful.

The yuccas (c) also have sword-like leaves, spine-tipped in some species. One of the most unusual is *Yucca whipplei* (Z9) which has a globe-shaped arrangement of viciously spine-tipped greyish-green leaves. *Y. filamentosa* (Z5) is better known, forming a clump of green leaves edged with white cotton-like filaments. It has some variegated varieties: 'Variegata' and 'Bright Edge'. Another popular yucca is *Y. flaccida* (Z6) whose leaf edges also have cotton-like filaments. Try to obtain the variety 'Ivory' as this flowers well. All the yuccas, incidentally, produce tall stems in summer carrying white or cream lily-like flowers, generally only when they are very well established.

Some yuccas produce a tree-like stem topped with leaves, including *Y. gloriosa* (Adam's Needle) (Z6) with viciously spine-tipped leaves and *Y. glauca* (Z6) with greyish foliage. The yuccas are generally quite hardy given a sheltered, well-drained site.

Not so hardy is the yucca-like *Beschorneria yuccoides* (Z8)(c). This has greyish-green sword-like leaves and, when well-established, a tall reddish stem bearing conspicuous red bracts and pendulous, tubular green flowers.

Two cordylines (Cabbage Palms) (Z8)(c) can be grown out of doors if winters are not too severe. They have evergreen sword-like leaves. *C. australis* eventually produces a branching trunk topped with greyish-green leaves, or purple-flushed in variety 'Purpurea'. *C. indivisa* also forms a trunk eventually, but it does not branch, carrying long green leaves. The cordylines are particularly suitable for mild coastal gardens.

Kniphofias (Red Hot Pokers) (c) with handsome grassy foliage and bold spikes of red, orange, yellow or cream flowers in late summer and autumn not only add colour in the gravel area but also contrast well in shape with many of the other plants. Undoubtedly the most dramatic is *K. caulescens* (Z7) which makes large clumps of broad grey-green leaves up to 1m (3ft) in length. It produces spikes of salmon-red flowers in autumn which gradually change to yellow. In cold areas the crowns will need protecting in winter with bracken or straw.

There are several very hardy ornamental grasses (c) which grow well in gravel areas. With clumps of thin blue-grey foliage are *Helictotrichon sempervirens* and *Festuca glauca*, both small grasses for the front of the bed. Contrasting beautifully with these in colour is *Deschampsia caespitosa* 'Bronze Veil' with unusual bronze-coloured flowers. Taller grasses include several miscanthus species like the 3m (10ft) tall *M. sacchariflorus* with arching green foliage, the gold-banded *M. sinensis* 'Zebrinus' and the variegated *M. s.* 'Variegatus'. If space permits it is worth including the very wide-spreading *Cortaderia selloana* (Pampas Grass) (Z7), noted for its silver plumes in autumn. There is, however, a dwarf form called 'Pumila'.

Eryngium (c) is a diverse genus containing some really unusual and exotic-looking plants which resemble tropical bromeliads and agaves. For instance, *Eryngium agavifolium* (Z8) produces a large rosette of long, sword-like, spine-edged leaves and globular green flowers on 1.5m (5ft) stems. *E. bromeliifolium* (Z8) also forms a rosette of long spine-edged leaves and similar flower heads.

A SCREE GARDEN FOR ALPINES
Another idea for a sunny well-drained area in the modern urban plot is a scree garden for displaying alpines or rock plants. It is more economical and often a more realistic proposition than a rock garden.

An unusual idea for a sunny well-drained area in a modern urban plot is the scree garden for displaying alpines or rock plants. It is more economical and often a more realistic proposition than a rock garden. The scree should be created on a slight slope, say between two rock outcrops, to resemble a drift of broken rock. Many alpines are suited to a scree garden, such as androsace species (a), dianthus or Alpine Pinks, (b), and Phyteuma comosum (c) with unusual bottle-shaped flowers

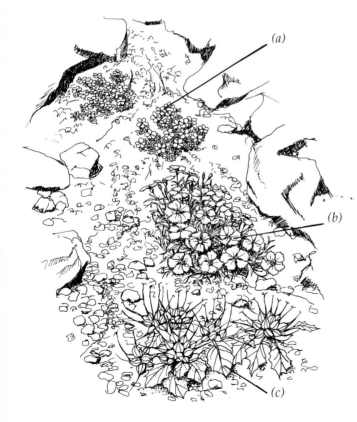

(a)

(b)

(c)

Ideally the scree should be created on a slight slope to resemble a drift of broken rock at the base of a cliff (which is what a scree is in nature). Conditions in a natural scree are very poor as there is virtually no soil or humus, yet many plants thrive, rooting deeply in search of moisture and nutrients. A scree in the garden is the ideal place to grow those alpines which demand very well-drained conditions, although they should not be subjected to quite such a lean diet as in nature.

The scree garden should be of irregular shape and is built direct on the soil. Make up a compost of one part loam, one part peat, one part coarse horticultural sand and ten parts stone chippings (or pea shingle). Enrich this with slow-release organic fertiliser. With this compost make up a bed at least 30cm (12in) deep, retaining the edges with rocks if necessary.

If your garden soil is not very well drained you should first place a 10cm (4in) layer of rubble or broken bricks over the ground before adding the compost as this will considerably improve drainage. After planting the scree cover the compost with a layer of stone chippings. If available you can incorporate a few well-shaped pieces of rock into the bed, partially sinking them into the compost.

Choice alpines

Having created such perfect conditions for alpines, select some of the more choice plants rather than common, often rampant kinds. A good alpine nurseryman will be able to supply them; they are not the sort of plants that you will find in garden centres. (Alpines can also be grown in pots or pans.)

Androsace (Bog Rosemary) species (Z6) are suitable, such as *A. hedraeantha* or *A. sempervivoides* which form rosettes and produce pink flowers in spring. Several campanula (Bellflower) species (Z5) are suitable, such as *C. alpina* with blue flowers in summer, and *C. pulla* with dark violet-purple bells in summer. Dianthus (Pinks) (Z5) are essential scree-garden plants. Try *D. arvernensis* with brilliant pink blooms, or *D. myrtinervis*, a little gem with pink blooms set against creeping mats of foliage. All flower in summer.

Draba (Whitlow Grass) species (Z5) form tiny dense domes of foliage studded with yellow flowers in spring. Some good species include *D. aizoides* and *D. longisiliqua*. The alpine hebes (Z6) from New Zealand are well worth growing and there are many

to choose from, including *H. buchananii* with grey foliage and *H. vernicosa* with glossy deep green leaves. Both have white flowers in summer.

The summer-flowering alpine penstemons (Z8) are ideal for a scree, like *P. roezlii* with blue flowers and the bright pink *P. rupicola* whose blooms are set against greyish-green leaves. An unusual plant for the scree is *Phyteuma comosum* (Z5) which produces stemless heads of purplish bottle-shaped blooms during the summer.

There are several dwarf potentillas (Cinquefoils) (Z6) with yellow flowers in summer rather like tiny single roses. *P. cuneata* is a mat-forming plant with light yellow blooms, thriving in the poorest well-drained soils.

The raoulias (Z7) from New Zealand are essentially foliage plants, forming neat mats of minute leaves. Forming conspicuous silvery mats is the best-known species, *R. hookeri* (syn. *R. australis). R. lutescens* forms greyish-green mats which in spring are covered with minute yellow flowers.

Silene acaulis (Moss Campion) (Z2) is a mat-forming plant which is studded with bright pink starry flowers in late spring and early summer. There are several alpine veronicas, but some are invasive and best avoided. However, *V. selleri* can be recommended as it forms compact clumps which produce little spikes of deep blue flowers in summer

This selection of scree-garden plants will, hopefully, whet your appetite. There are many other alpines which are suitable for this feature.

WARM SUNNY WALLS

Walls which receive full sun and which are well sheltered from cold winds can provide a home for many choice plants, including climbers and wall shrubs. Many of these have a very exotic appearance and indeed are often quite tender, being suitable for outdoor cultivation only in mild parts of the country. Many fruits can also be grown on warm sunny walls, including such exotic kinds as peaches, nectarines, grapes, figs, apricots and kiwi fruit (Chinese Gooseberry).

In the nineteenth century, when there was great interest in trained fruit trees, fruits were often grown on serpentine or crinkle-crankle walls. Such walls, built on an undulating plan and specially constructed for fruit growing, provided sheltered niches which encouraged optimum growth and ripening. Some serpentine walls still exist in old gardens and should

be preserved at all costs. They can still be used, of course, for growing fruits, tender climbers and wall shrubs.

Some walls can reflect heat, especially those painted white or some other light colour, and this can create very hot conditions indeed. One way to get over this is to paint the wall a darker colour, such as terracotta or dark grey. Heat will then be absorbed rather than reflected. Natural brickwork (walls built of red or terracotta-colour bricks) absorbs quite a lot of heat which is of benefit to the plants as it ensures a warmer microclimate around them.

A border immediately in front of a wall, in which the climbers and so on are planted, can remain extremely dry as the wall deflects rain. Therefore never plant hard up against the wall, but position plants at least 30cm (12in) away from it. They will then stand more chance of receiving moisture during rainfall and will consequently establish and grow very much better.

Before planting climbers, wall shrubs and fruits dig the border thoroughly and incorporate a good quantity of bulky organic matter into each trench,

such as well-rotted farmyard manure or garden compost. These materials will help to ensure moist conditions.

Climbers and wall shrubs

Full use should be made of walls for growing plants for they represent a considerable amount of additional space in a garden. Generally there is no reason why walls should not be fully covered with climbing plants and wall shrubs. Contrary to popular belief climbers will not cause any harm to sound brickwork, although tall kinds can grow into gutters, causing blockage, and can even grow under tiles and lift them. The plants should be pruned back before they reach this stage.

The term 'wall shrub' is used to describe a shrub which is best grown against a wall, for protection. It is not trained in any way, just left to grow naturally. Climbers, on the other hand, are trained to their supports by spacing out and tying in the stems as necessary. Suitable supports include timber trellis panels or plastic-coated steel mounted on the wall, about 5cm (2in) away from it, or a series of taut,

horizontal galvanised or plastic-coated wires, also held the same distance from the wall. This gap allows air circulation behind the plants.

A popular wall shrub is *Abelia floribunda* (Z9) which is on the tender side and needs very warm sheltered conditions. This late-spring to mid-summer flowering evergreen has somewhat tubular bright pink blooms in profusion and is seen to perfection in sheltered western gardens.

The abutilons (c) are also wall shrubs and really only recommended for mild regions. Elsewhere they make superb conservatory specimens. Best-known is *A. megapotamicum* (Z9), an evergreen shrub with dangling, bell-shaped yellow and red flowers in summer and autumn. Very showy and unusual is *A. x suntense* 'Jermyns' (Z8) with large, rounded, deep mauve flowers in summer. *A. vitifolium* (Z8) can also be grown out of doors in favoured regions and usually varieties are chosen: 'Tennant's White' (pure white) and 'Veronica Tennant' (mauve) both have large saucer-like flowers and attractive greyish leaves. It is recommended that the abutilons are protected from frost in winter with bracken or straw.

Only suited to mild regions, the spring-flowering acacias (Wattles) (c) are superb wall shrubs. Elsewhere they should be grown in cool conservatories. They are evergreen and produce clusters of yellow flowers, and are best grown in acid soils. *Acacia dealbata* (Mimosa) (Z8) has very ferny silvery foliage and golden-yellow flowers.

An unusual wall shrub is *Adenocarpus decorticans* (Z9), which is in the pea family and bears yellow pea flowers in late spring and early summer. The ferny foliage is deciduous. It is not considered reliably hardy in cold areas.

Aristolochia (Dutchman's Pipe) is quite an exotic-looking genus, of which the species *A. durior* (Z6) is best known. It is a deciduous climber with flowers shaped rather like a pipe, hence the common name. They come in a combination of brown, yellow and green and are produced in summer.

Bignonia capreolata (syn. *Doxantha capreolata)* (c) is suited to outdoor cultivation only in mild regions (Z9). It is an evergreen climber clinging by means of tendrils and produces striking orange-red tubular flowers in early summer. Rather similar, and indeed related, is *Campsis radicans* (Trumpet Vine) (Z5) which blooms in late summer. It has vivid orange and red trumpet-shaped flowers and clings by means of aerial roots. Also worth growing is the

(b)

(a)

hybrid *C. x tagliabuana* 'Madame Galen' with pinky red blooms.

Among the most popular wall shrubs are the ceanothus (Z7)(c). The evergreen kinds are the most attractive, producing masses of flowers in all shades of blue in the spring or summer. Some particularly good hybrids include 'Cascade', 'Delight' and 'Southmead'.

Cestrum parqui (Z9)(c) is only suitable for mild gardens and even then can be cut back by hard frosts, although generally it produces new growth from ground level in the spring. In cold areas grow it in a cool conservatory. It is a deciduous shrub which produces clusters of tubular yellow flowers in summer and early autumn. Cut back any frost-damaged stems in spring.

Often grown outdoors in mild areas, and in conservatories in colder regions, is the climber *Clianthus puniceus* (Parrot's Bill) (Z8)(c) with attractive ferny evergreen foliage and parrot-bill-like deep red flowers in late spring and early summer. Protect the base of the plant from frost in winter with bracken or straw.

A large established plant of *Fremontodendron californicum* (Z8)(c) is a beautiful sight from late spring onwards when bedecked with large golden-yellow bowl-shaped flowers. Deciduous or partially evergreen, this wall shrub is only suited to mild gardens. A hybrid worth searching for is

*Walls which receive full sun and which are well
sheltered from cold winds can provide a home for many
choice climbers and wall shrubs, such as abutilons.*
A. x suntense *'Jermyns' (a) has large, rounded, deep
mauve flowers in summer, and*
A. megapotamicum *(b) produces dangling,
bell-shaped, yellow and red blooms in summer and
autumn*

The evergreen shrub Magnolia grandiflora *(a),
with huge cream flowers in summer and autumn
can cover a large sunny wall in time. A good
companion for this is the Blue Passion Flower,*
Passiflora caerulea *(b), a vigorous evergreen climber*

(a)

(b)

'California Glory' with larger flowers.

Highly fragrant white flowers are produced during summer by *Jasminum polyanthum*, while *J. mesnyi* has yellow blooms in spring. Both of these climbing jasmines are only suitable for gardens in mild regions (Z8) and would appreciate some frost protection with bracken or straw during the winter.(c).

With the ability to cover a large wall given time is the evergreen *Magnolia grandiflora* (Z7). This wall shrub has large thick shiny leaves and when well established produces bowl-shaped cream flowers almost 30cm (12in) across in summer and autumn. Try to obtain one of the forms like 'Exmouth' or 'Goliath' as these start to bloom at an earlier age.

For mild gardens only, or cool conservatories in colder areas, is the climber *Mandevilla suaveolens* (Chilean Jasmine) (Z9)(c), valued for its highly scented white flowers in summer. The climbing *Mutisia oligodon* (Climbing Gazania) (Z9)(c) is a bit hardier although in a hard winter the top growth may be killed; however, the plant usually produces new shoots from the base in spring. It bears pink daisy-like flowers in summer and autumn.

Of the passion flowers, *Passiflora caerulea* (Blue Passion Flower) (Z8)(c) is the hardiest, but again is only suited to mild areas. It is a vigorous evergreen climber producing a succession of blue and white flowers in summer and autumn. It is best to protect the base of the plant with bracken or straw during

winter. Top growth may be killed back during severe weather, but new growth is usually produced in spring.

Senecio scandens (Z8) is a semi-evergreen climber with many small yellow daisy-like flowers in autumn (c). It is excellent for twining through a larger wall shrub such as solanum.

Except in the mildest regions (Z9), *Tecomaria capensis* (c) should be grown in a cool conservatory. It is an evergreen climber with vivid scarlet trumpets towards the end of summer.

The hardiest of the climbing solanums is *S. crispum* (Chilean Potato Tree) (Z8). It is semi-evergreen, and produces a succession of purplish-blue potato-like flowers throughout summer and early autumn. The variety 'Glasnevin' is hardier.

A self-clinging climber, *Trachelospermum asiaticum* (Z7) is an evergreen with highly fragrant cream-white flowers in summer. Also with highly fragrant white flowers in summer is the climber *Wattakaka sinensis* (Z9).The attractive leaves are covered with grey 'felt' on the undersides. Both are (c).

Fruits

Growing fruits in sheltered conditions on warm sunny walls has several advantages. Not only can the more exotic kinds be grown, but they are also more easily cared for. It is a comparatively simple matter to drape netting in front of trained fruits to

protect the ripening fruits from the ravages of birds, which are partial to many kinds such as cherries, currants and pears. Also, some fruit trees bloom early in the year, particularly peaches, nectarines and some apples, and their flowers are liable to be damaged by frosts. They can be protected by draping fine-mesh netting or hessian in front of them at night when a frost is forecast. Fruits can also be grown in tubs.

APPLES

Apples (Z6-9) can be grown as espaliers which consist of a central stem from which pairs of horizontal branches grow, spaced about 45cm (18in) apart. The trees are perfectly flat against the wall and the branches are trained to horizontal wires. Each branch is encouraged to form fruiting spurs by pruning back all the lateral shoots to within three leaves of their base in mid-summer each year. Leading shoots are also cut back to restrict spread. Usually espaliers are grown on dwarfing rootstocks and can be spaced about 3.6m (12ft) apart.

More trees can be grown in the available space if the cordon system is chosen. The cordon consists of a single stem with fruiting spurs along its length (these are encouraged by pruning as described for the espalier). The trees are planted 75-90cm (2½-3ft) apart at an angle of 45° and trained to canes and horizontal wires.

Make sure you grow several varieties of apple together so that they cross-pollinate. They must, of course, flower at the same time and be compatible. Suitable varieties for growing together are indicated in fruit-growers' catalogues and also on the labels in garden centres.

Flowers should be protected from late frosts and fruits from birds.

APRICOTS

Apricots (Z8-10) ripen their fruits between mid-summer and early autumn. They are best grown as fan-trained specimens planted 4.5m (15ft) apart and

Warm sunny walls are perfect for growing climbing and rambling roses, for colour in the summer. Here is the old but still popular climber 'Cécile Brunner'. The yellow-flowered Fremontodendron californicum *is growing alongside*
(SAVILL GARDENS, THE GREAT PARK, WINDSOR, BERKSHIRE)

trained to horizontal wires. The fan consists of a short trunk from which radiates a system of branches in the shape of a fan. The fruits are carried on laterals, and in mid-summer each year the tips of these are nipped out. After fruiting, the laterals are cut back by half their length. Leading shoots have to be cut back by a quarter each year in spring.

As apricots are self-compatible only one tree need be grown, but the flowers will need pollinating by hand, using a soft brush, as they appear early in the year before pollinating insects are about. The flowers should be protected from frosts.

CHERRIES

Sweet cherries (Z6-9) are popular fruits for wall training and are grown as fans (see Apricots, above). Cherries are large vigorous trees, but are now available on dwarfing rootstocks which are more suitable for small gardens and limited space. Plant them 4-5m (15ft) apart. If you have space for only one tree then plant a self-compatible variety such as 'Stella'.

A fan-trained cherry needs annual pruning. In mid-summer lateral shoots are cut back to six leaves, and leading shoots may need shortening when they start to grow above the wall. In early autumn further prune back the laterals to within three leaves of their base. Fruit buds will then form at the base of these spurs. Flowers must be protected from frost and the fruits and winter buds from birds.

CURRANTS

Red and white currants (Z6-9) are best grown as cordons – a single-stemmed plant with fruiting laterals. They are planted in a row, 30-38cm (12-15in) apart, and trained to canes and horizontal wires.

Annual pruning of the cordon is quite simple: in mid-summer all lateral shoots are pruned back to within four or five leaves of their base. Only prune the leading shoot when it has reached the required height. Then in winter further reduce the laterals to 2.5cm (1in). The leader can also be pruned back, but leave some new wood.

Protect flowers from frost and fruits and winter buds from birds.

FIGS

Figs (Z8) can be successfully grown out of doors in cool temperate regions, when they will set one crop of fruits per year. The tree is best grown as a fan and trained to horizontal wires, and as the tree is very

On a warm sunny wall apples (shown here) and pears can be grown as espaliers. The trees are trained to horizontal wires and are perfectly flat against the wall.

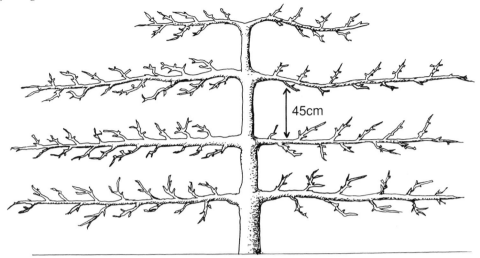

45cm

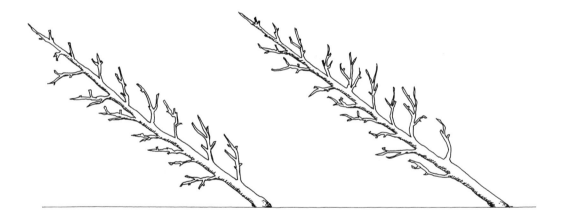

ABOVE

Apples (shown here) and pears can also be grown as cordons, planted at an angle of 45 degrees. More trees can be grown in the available space with this system. Currants and gooseberries can also be grown as cordons, which are trained to a system of horizontal wires attached to the wall

LEFT

Lateral shoots of a cordon or espalier apple should be pruned back to within three leaves of their base in summer to encourage fruiting spurs. Pears are pruned in the same way

vigorous the roots will need restricting, as discussed under Patio Planting, (p.80). Alternatively, grow it in a tub.

When pruning a fan-trained fig bear in mind that the fruits are produced at the tips of shoots formed during the previous summer and overwinter as tiny pea-sized fruitlets. They ripen in late summer and early autumn. The main framework of branches of the fan produces many lateral shoots. In mid-summer cut out the tips of every alternate shoot. This encourages the production of more shoots, carrying embryo fruits. In late autumn half the laterals which produced fruits are cut back to within 2.5cm (1in) of their base. Bear in mind that lateral shoots should be spaced 20-30cm (8-12in) apart, so remove any surplus shoots. Lateral shoots should be tied in as necessary to the wires.

Protect young fruits and shoots from frost over the winter by lightly covering the tree with bracken or straw, holding it in place with plastic netting.

GOOSEBERRIES

Gooseberries (Z6-9) are best trained as cordons in exactly the same way as currants. Protect the flowers from frost and the fruits and winter buds from birds.

Sweet cherries are popular fruits for wall training and are grown as fans, trained to horizontal wires. Other fruits which can be fan-trained are apricots, figs, nectarines, peaches, plums and quinces

GRAPES

Grape vines (Z8-10) can be grown successfully outdoors in all but the coldest regions provided the hardier white varieties are chosen. Use the rod and spur system of training, spacing plants 1.2m (4ft) apart. This system consists of a single vertical stem with fruiting spurs and support is by means of horizontal wires. Pruning involves cutting back all lateral shoots (produced the previous summer) to within one bud of their base in early winter. In spring new shoots will be produced from these spurs. They will produce flower trusses and should be pinched out at two leaves beyond the trusses. Tie in the shoots horizontally to the wires. The leading shoot can be cut back in summer when it reaches the top of the wall. It can be reduced further in early winter, leaving some new wood

Allow only one bunch of grapes per spur. If they are being grown for dessert thin out the bunches when the berries are pea-sized, giving the remainder room to swell. The fruits ripen in the autumn.

KIWI FRUIT

The kiwi fruit or Chinese Gooseberry *(Actinidia chinensis)* is a vigorous perennial climber with furry brown fruits ripening in mid-autumn. It can be

successfully grown outdoors in all but the coldest regions (Z8), but needs a long warm summer for successful fruiting. Fruits are borne on female plants and need to be pollinated by a male plant. Plant them 3-4m (10-15ft) apart and support by means of horizontal wires.

Newly planted specimens are cut back to within 30cm (12in) of the ground. The resulting shoots are then trained horizontally to the wires. Cut out the tips when they have filled the available space. Shoots which carry fruits should be cut back to six or seven leaves beyond the fruit. Any laterals not carrying fruits can be cut back to five leaves during the summer. When growth becomes congested carry out winter pruning by cutting back laterals which are three years old to within a bud of their base.

NECTARINES

The nectarine (Z8-10) is self-compatible and therefore a single tree can be grown, ideally as a fan (see Apricots (p.95). Pruning of the fan is quite simple and the aim is for a succession of new fruit-bearing lateral shoots. Fruits are carried on shoots formed

Figs can be successfully grown out of doors in cool temperate regions, when they will set one crop of fruits per year, ripening in late summer or early autumn

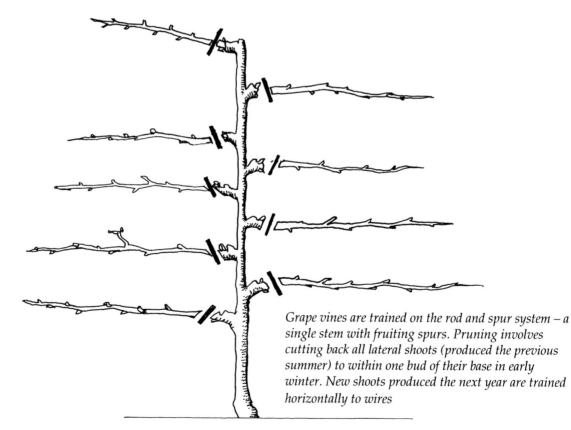

Grape vines are trained on the rod and spur system – a single stem with fruiting spurs. Pruning involves cutting back all lateral shoots (produced the previous summer) to within one bud of their base in early winter. New shoots produced the next year are trained horizontally to wires

the previous summer. Annual pruning in early autumn consists of cutting back lateral shoots that carried fruits. Cut them back to where new shoots have formed: these will replace the ones removed and bear fruits in the summer.

Flowers should be pollinated by hand as they appear early in the year before pollinating insects are about. Use a soft brush. Protect flowers from frost. Choose early varieties for outdoor cultivation.

PEACHES

These are grown in exactly the same way as nectarines (Z8-10). The nectarine, in fact, is a 'sport' or mutation of the peach.

PEARS

Pears (Z6-9) are grown in exactly the same way as apples (p.95). Make sure you grow several varieties together so that they cross-pollinate, choosing compatible varieties.

PLUMS

Plums (Z6-9) are grown as fan-trained specimens in exactly the same way as apricots . Choose trees on semi-dwarfing rootstocks to avoid excessively vigorous growth.

Protect flowers from frost, and protect fruits and winter buds from birds. If you want only one tree choose a self-compatible variety. It may need hand-pollinating if there are few insects about.

QUINCE

The Quince (Cydonia oblonga) (Z5) needs a good warm summer for the fruits to ripen thoroughly, which takes place in mid-to late autumn. It can be trained as a fan.

The annual summer pruning of the fan is aimed at encouraging fruiting spurs. The lateral shoots are pruned back to three or four leaves in mid-summer. Leading shoots can be cut back to restrict spread. Spurs eventually become too long and can then be cut back into old wood during winter.

All of the fruits mentioned here can be bought partially trained by the nurseryman. You will need to further train the basic framework of branches or stems to cover the allotted wall space. This means allowing leading shoots to grow to fill the space, and possibly encouraging further branches in the

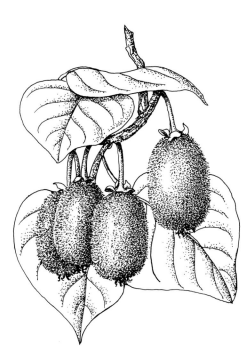

The Kiwi Fruit or Chinese Gooseberry (Actinidia chinensis) *needs a long warm summer for successful fruiting, but it can be successfully grown out of doors in all but the coldest regions. It produces furry brown fruits*

The quince (Cydonia oblonga) *is very hardy, but needs a good warm summer for the large fragrant yellow fruits to ripen thoroughly. They should mature in mid- to late autumn*

case of such forms as espaliers and fans. During the formative period it is best to lightly prune back leading shoots each year, leaving some of the new wood. This encourages laterals and fruiting spurs.

WALL BORDERS

Having covered the warm sunny wall with climbers, wall shrubs and fruits, consider next the border in front of it. Very often this is quite a narrow border and, provided the drainage is impeccable, makes an ideal home for bulbs, small shrubs and perennials, including the many charming silver-leaved plants. Some of these bulbs and other plants are on the tender side and often the sheltered warm border fronting a south-facing wall is the only place to grow them.

Bulbs

Starting with the most tender bulbs, nerines are among the most popular and valued for their autumn flowers. *N. bowdenii* (Z8)(c) is the only one grown outdoors in temperate climates and generally survives quite severe winters. It produces stems up to 60cm (2ft) high bearing heads of pink flowers with reflexed petals. Later the long strap-shaped leaves appear.

Eucomis comosa (Pineapple Flower) (Z8)(c) has broad lance-shaped leaves up to 60cm (2ft) long and 90cm (3ft) high purple-spotted stems bearing heads of fragrant, yellowish-green, lily-like flowers. Flowering starts in early autumn, although sometimes flowers may appear in late summer. In cold regions protect plants over winter by covering with a mound of coarse sand. Also autumn-flowering is *Amaryllis belladonna* (Z6)(c) with large pink trumpet-shaped flowers carried on 60cm (2ft) high stems. These are followed by long strap-shaped leaves. Again, this bulb will survive quite severe winters, but it is advisable to cover the young leaves with straw or bracken to protect them from frost.

Related to amaryllis is the summer- to autumn-flowering *Crinum x powellii* (Z6)(c) with large pink trumpet-shaped flowers carried on 45cm (18in) high stems. Long strap-shaped leaves are produced. Protect young growth from frost with a light covering of bracken or straw.

Several gladioli (c) are fully hardy in cool temperate regions, such as *G. byzantinus* with purplish-red flowers and *G. imbricatus* with deep purple blooms.

Both grow to about 45cm (18in) in height and bloom in mid-summer.

The onion family has some attractive hardy ornamental species such as *Allium moly*, with bright yellow starry flowers, and *A. karataviense*, noted for its broad greyish-green leaves with a metallic sheen and large globular heads of white flowers with a hint of mauve. Both are dwarf bulbs and bloom in early summer (c).

The many crocus species (Z6)(c) are suitable for the front of this border. There are so many that it is difficult to choose, but aim for flowering at different seasons. For instance, blooming in autumn are *Crocus speciosus* (bluish mauve), and *C. nudiflorus* (white and purple). Blooming in winter are *C. laevigatus fontenayi* (purple and cream), and *C. chrysanthus* varieties in various colour. Popular spring-flowering crocuses include *C. minimus* (yellow and purple), and *C. aureus* (deep orange-yellow).

With bright yellow crocus-like flowers and handsome deep green strap-shaped foliage is *Sternbergia lutea* (Z6) which blooms in the autumn. The deep yellow *S. clusiana* (Z6) is also well worth growing. Both are suited to the front of the border. (c).

As with crocuses, there are many tulip species (Z5)(c) to choose from which flower in late winter and spring. Many are dwarf, suitable for the front of the border, like *Tulipa biflora* (white with a yellow centre), *T. clusiana* (white with red tints), *T. greigii* (orange-red), *T. kaufmanniana* (white, red and yellow), and *T. tarda* (white with a yellow centre).

Silver-foliage plants

Some charming effects can be created by growing the bulbs described above with silver- or grey-leaved plants of dwarf stature, such as *Anthemis cupaniana* (Z8), a perennial with feathery grey foliage and a long succession of white daisy flowers in summer. All are suitable for containers.

There are several artemisia species (Z4) suited to our scheme, including *A. stelleriana*, a hardy perennial with deeply cut white foliage. The shrubby *A. schmidtiana* 'Nana' has beautiful silver-grey feathery foliage forming a neat mound, and is one of the best silver-foliage plants.

Ballota pseudodictamnus (Z8) is a dwarf shrub with woolly grey leaves and shoots. Protect it from excessive winter rains with a cloche.

Convolvulus cneorum (Z9) is best grown only in areas not subjected to very severe winters. It is an evergreen shrub with silky silvery leaves and white saucer-shaped flowers in summer. Cover it with a cloche in winter to protect it against excessive rain.

Only for mild regions is the evergreen shrub *Euryops pectinatus* (Z9) with grey foliage and shoots and deep yellow daisy flowers in late spring and early summer. Two shrubby helichrysums are worth growing, but only in mild areas (Z8): *H. angustifolium* (Curry Plant) has narrow silver leaves, and *H. splendidum* has woolly silver-grey foliage. Both produce yellow flowers in summer.

Leucanthemum hosmariense (syn. *Chrysanthemum hosmariense*) (Z8) is a shrubby plant forming a low neat mound of silver-grey foliage and producing white daisy-like flowers in spring and summer. *Othonnopsis cheirifolia* (Z8) is a dwarf evergreen shrub which may not survive severe winters. It has grey-green paddle-shaped leaves and produces deep yellow daisy flowers in summer.

Hardier than many gardeners suppose is *Salvia argentea* (Silver Sage) (Z8), a short-lived perennial which forms a rosette of white woolly foliage. White flowers, with a hint of mauve, are carried on upright stems in summer. Cover with a cloche (open ends) in winter to protect against excessive rain.

Other 'treasures'

Several other plants are well worth including in this favoured border, including *Diascia rigescens* (c), a perennial with upright stems of rose-pink flowers from early summer to mid-autumn. It is not reliably hardy in cold regions, where young plants raised from cuttings are best overwintered under glass.

Haplopappus coronopifolius (c) is a hardy perennial forming a mound of evergreen finely divided foliage and producing orange daisy-like flowers in summer and autumn. Valued for its winter flowers is *Iris unguicularis* (syn. *I. stylosa*) (Algerian Iris) (Z5), a hardy perennial with evergreen grassy foliage and pale blue flowers.

The osteospermums (c) were previously known as dimorphothecas and are popularly called African Daisies. They are low-growing perennials pro-

A well-drained border in front of a sunny wall makes an ideal home for bulbous plants. An autumn-flowering selection could consist of Nerine bowdenii *(a);* Crocus speciosus *(b);* Eucomis comosa *(c), the dramatic Pineapple Flower; and* Amaryllis belladonna *(d)*

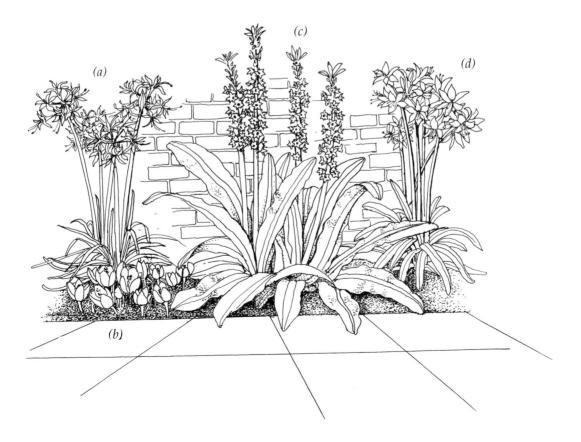

ducing daisy-like flowers in summer. Two species are hardy enough to be grown outside except perhaps in regions with very hard winters. *O. barberiae* 'Compacta' has large rose-purple flowers, and *O. ecklonis* 'Prostrata' bears white flowers with deep blue centres flushed with blue on the reverse (both Z8).

Schizostylis coccinea (Z8) is a herbaceous perennial with grassy foliage, valued for its bright red autumn flowers. There are varieties in shades of red and pink. Add plenty of peat to the soil before planting and in cold regions protect plants over winter with a covering of bracken or straw. (c).

The shrubby zauschnerias (Californian Fuchsias) (Z8)(c) produce red tubular fuchsia-like flowers in summer and autumn. *Z. californica* and *Z. cana* are similar, with grey-green leaves. In cold regions cover with straw or bracken in the winter to give some protection against hard frosts. The stems should be pruned down almost to soil level in early spring.

SHRUB OR MIXED BORDERS

The main planting areas in many gardens are mixed borders where a variety of plants is grown in harmony, such as shrubs, perennials and bulbs. Borders devoted purely to shrubs are also quite popular and certainly very labour-saving.

If these borders receive full sun, are very well sheltered from wind (ideally backed by a hedge or

RIGHT
Silver-foliage plants are an excellent choice for hot dry areas, either in narrow borders at the front of warm walls, or in other parts of the garden. They combine well with many other plants, including bulbs. Pink-flowered plants, for instance, associate especially well with silver foliage (PREEN MANOR, SHROPSHIRE)

BELOW
Silver- or grey-leaved plants are ideal for a well-drained border in front of a warm sunny wall and make ideal companions for bulbs. Popular examples of silver or grey plants include Ballota pseudodictamnus *(a);* Helichrysum angustifolium *(b), the Curry Plant; and* Artemisia schmidtiana 'Nana' *(c). A dramatic Ornamental Onion,* Allium karataviense *(d), has been included in this scheme. It has broad greyish-green leaves and large heads of white flowers in early summer*

fence) and the soil is very well-drained, you have an ideal home for many of the less-hardy shrubs. Most of these are only recommended for mild regions. This certainly applies to the Australian and New Zealand shrubs, of which there is now a considerable range available. Gardeners in colder or exposed regions should consider some of these for cultivation in the cool conservatory.

Shrubs from Australia and New Zealand
While many of these need to be grown in a cool conservatory to protect them from frost, there are, nevertheless, quite a few suitable for growing outdoors in mild regions. Some are quite well-known; others many people have yet to discover for hitherto they have not been readily available.

Perhaps best-known is callistemon (Bottle Brush), (Z8) medium-sized evergreen shrubs with bottle-brush-like flowers in summer (c). The hardiest species is *C. subulatus* with crimson flowers. It is very much like *C. linearis*, which has brilliant red blooms. Flowers in this colour are also borne by *C. citrinus* 'Splendens' which has greyish-green foliage. With light yellow flowers is *C. salignus*.

The evergreen grevilleas (Z8) are also mainly medium-sized shrubs. Those described here have needle-like leaves and summer flowers which look something like those of Honeysuckle (lonicera). Freely producing red flowers is *G. rosmarinifolia*, while *G. sulphurea* has light yellow blooms and is the hardiest species. Grevilleas need to be grown in acid or lime-free soil (c).

Grown for its handsome yellowy-green leathery evergreen leaves is the large shrub *Griselinia littoralis* (Z7)(c). This is an excellent choice for maritime gardens, where it is often grown as a hedge, as it tolerates salt spray. The variety 'Variegata' has variegated green and white foliage.

Among the best-known of all New Zealand shrubs are the evergreen hebes (Shrubby Veronicas) (c), ranging from small to medium-sized and large shrubs. In the summer they produce a long succession of flowers, which are generally carried in spikes. In mild or well-sheltered cooler areas they are indispensable shrubs for borders.

Some well-known small to medium-sized hebes include *H. albicans* (Z7) with very attractive grey-green leaves, which are perhaps more showy than the white flowers. *H. armstrongii* (Z7) is one of the whipcord hebes with minute cypress-like leaves in yellow-green, and white flowers. This is basically a foliage shrub, as is another whipcord species, *H. cupressoides* (Z7), with greyish-green foliage and light blue flowers. These whipcord hebes make marvellous companions for many other shrubs with normal rounded or lanceolate leaves.

Hebe brachysiphon (Z6) has conspicuous white flowers set against deep green foliage. Contrary to popular belief, *H. hulkeana* (Z8) should be grown in a border rather than against a wall as here it benefits from better air circulation which reduces incidence of disease. Flower colour varies from shades of blue to lilac and white.

Hebe salicifolia (Z7) has light green foliage and white flowers with a hint of mauve. It is often grown in seaside gardens. *H. speciosa* (Z7) bears handsome shiny deep green foliage and conspicuous spikes of purple flowers. There are many hybrids of hebe varying in hardiness and they are also well worth considering for mild or well-sheltered gardens.

Leptospermums (Z9)(c) are now becoming better-known and are highly recommended for mild gardens and very sheltered sites in cooler areas. They are evergreen, and the following are medium-sized to large shrubs. They bear masses of small flowers, rather like tiny single roses, in spring and summer. *L. cunninghamii* is one of the hardiest species with greyish foliage and sprays of white flowers. *L. flavescens* also has white flowers, or they may be tinted with yellow. Very attractive is *L. lanigerum* with silvery foliage and white flowers, which is one of the hardiest species. *L. scoparium* also has white flowers, but there are many forms in other colours, like 'Keatleyi' with comparatively large pink flowers; 'Nichollsii Grandiflorum' with bright red flowers and deep purple-bronze leaves; and 'Red Damask' with double dark red blooms.

The olearias (Daisy Bushes) (Z8)(c) are excellent evergreen shrubs for coastal gardens and sheltered gardens inland. On the coast they tolerate salt spray and some are used for hedging. They produce white or cream daisy-like flowers in the summer. Often the foliage is white-felted below. There are many species, including *O. avicenniifolia* with scented flowers, one of the best for hedging; *O.* x *haastii*, also recommended for hedging, with scented flowers; *O. ilicifolia*, with tough greyish-green leaves and scented flowers; *O. macrodonta* 'Major' (New Zealand Holly), with leaves like those of holly and scented blooms, making a good hedging plant; *O.* x *scilloniensis*, only for mild gardens, with grey foliage, free-flowering; *O. stellulata* 'Splendens', only for mild areas, with blue flowers; and *O. traversii*, used mainly as a hedge or windbreak in coastal gardens, the most attractive feature being the glossy leaves and woolly white shoots.

The pittosporums (Z8)(c) are very handsome evergreen shrubs grown for their attractive foliage. The following are medium to large shrubs, ideal for mild coastal gardens and very sheltered places inland. Best-known of the pittosporums is undoubtedly *P. tenuifolium* with light green wavy-edged leaves and contrasting black twigs, which is one of the best species for hedging in mild areas. Small brown-purple sweetly scented flowers are produced in spring. There are several varieties including 'Purpureum' with purple foliage (one of the few purple-leaved evergreen shrubs); 'Silver Queen' with silver-grey foliage; and 'Variegatum' which has foliage edged with white.

Pittosporum crassifolium has white felt on the undersides of its longish leaves and reddish-purple

A border in full sun, very well sheltered from wind and with very well-drained soil, makes an ideal home for many of the less-hardy shrubs, such as those from New Zealand and Australia. Typical examples of southern hemisphere shrubs are Callistemon citrinus *'Splendens' (a), with red bottlebrush flowers;* Griselinia littoralis *(b), noted for its yellowish-green foliage; and* Hebe armstrongii *(c), one of the whipcord hebes with yellow-green foliage. They provide a pleasing composition with strong contrast in shape and texture*

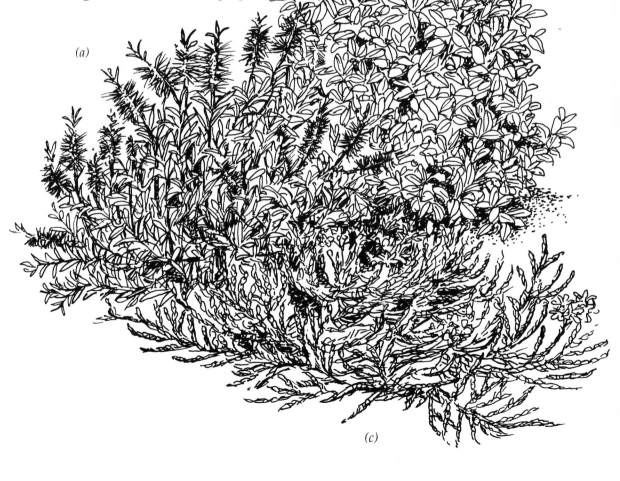

(a)

(b)

(c)

flowers in spring. It is good as a hedge in mild coastal gardens. *P. eugenioides* 'Variegatum' has white-edged foliage, and *P.* 'Garnettii' has grey-green leaves edged with white. Very distinctive is *P. tobira* with longish bright green leaves carried in whorls. The cream flowers have the fragrance of orange blossom. The variety 'Variegatum' has white-edged leaves.

Among the lesser-known plants from New Zealand are the carmichaelias (Butterfly Brooms), large and small, generally leafless shrubs of variable hardiness, most being rather tender and best attempted outdoors only in mild regions (Z9). The pea-like flowers are mainly white, marked with purple, and in many species are scented (c).

The species that are reasonably hardy include *Carmichaelia aligera*, a variable tallish species with flattened shoots and white and violet blooms; *C. glabrata*, a medium-sized shrub with upright heads of purple flowers; *C. ovata*, a fairly dwarf species whose blooms are flushed with purple; and, rather like *C. aligera*, the vigorous tall *C. solandri*.

The cassinias are basically foliage shrubs, rather heath-like in appearance, and in *C. fulvida* (Z8)(c), a small evergreen shrub, the foliage has a conspicuous golden hue.

The genus coprosma (c) from New Zealand is little-known. This is a group of variable evergreen shrubs, all rather tender and recommended for outdoor cultivation only in mild regions (Z8). They produce small flowers and the sexes are generally on separate plants, so both sexes have to be planted to ensure colourful berries, for which this genus is noted. Species worth trying include *C. acerosa* (Sand Coprosma), with prostrate habit and translucent blue berries; *C.* x *kirkii* 'Variegata', with sprawling habit and white-edged leaves; *C. repens*, with semi-prostrate habit and shiny deep green leaves, although there are several variegated varieties; *C. robusta*, a large shrub with orange-red berries; *C. robusta* 'Variegata', with yellow-variegated foliage; *C. rotundifolia*, with an upright habit, often reddish foliage and red berries; and *C. rugosa*, with a compact upright habit and white to light blue berries.

Several notospartiums (Pink Brooms) (c) from New Zealand are now available, including *N. carmicheliae* (Z8), a broom-like medium-sized leafless shrub with a weeping habit and smothered in pink pea-like flowers during mid-summer.

Several sophoras (c) come from New Zealand, including *S. tetraptera* (Z8), a large shrub or even a small tree, and *S. microphylla* (Z8), also a large shrub. Both have evergreen ferny foliage and carry clusters of large pea-like yellow flowers in late spring.

Other shrubs

There are several other shrubs from various parts of the world worth considering for the warm, well-drained, sheltered mixed or shrub border, including coronilla (c) which makes a cheerful show with bright yellow pea-like flowers throughout summer, set against ferny foliage. This is greyish in *C. glauca* (Z7), a medium-sized evergreen shrub. Hardier is *C. emerus* (Z6), the most popular species.

The escallonias, which are mainly evergreen, are excellent for mild coastal gardens and sheltered borders inland (Z7). By the sea they are often used as hedging, but make equally good border shrubs, producing red, pink or white flowers in summer. They vary in size from small to large.

Also in mild coastal gardens some of the hardy fuchsias are used for hedging, but again are equally suitable for the mixed or shrub border (c). They bloom over a long period in summer. The species normally grown outdoors is *F. magellanica* (Z6), a medium to large shrub with red and purple flowers. It has numerous varieties. In cold regions the stems may be killed back by frost, but new growth emerges from the crown in spring.

Indigofera gerardiana (Z8) is only suitable for mild climates. Of medium size, it has attractive ferny grey-green foliage and from mid-summer to mid-autumn produces pinkish purple pea-like flowers. *Spartium junceum* (Spanish Broom) (Z8) has leafless green stems and shoots, producing a succession of deep yellow pea-like flowers throughout summer. It is a large shrub, suitable for the back of the border.

Teucrium fruticans (Z8)(c) is a medium-sized half-hardy evergreen shrub only suitable for mild regions. It has attractive greyish aromatic foliage, a good background for the light blue flowers which are produced in succession from early summer to early autumn. Make sure this shrub has a really sheltered position.

RIGHT
The Cabbage Palm Cordyline australis *makes an excellent 'dot' plant for bedding in cool temperate climates, especially in milder areas where it may survive the winter*

Scented Air

The sheltered garden is the perfect place for growing fragrant plants. In a windy garden flower and foliage scents are quickly wafted away and can be virtually unnoticeable, but in wind-free conditions they linger on the air. Often, when the weather is warm, leaf scents are more pronounced, too. Furthermore, in a sheltered garden butterflies and bees are more likely to search out their favourite scented plants.

Make the most of fragrant plants, especially in secluded sitting areas where scents can be enjoyed at leisure. Drape an arbour, gazebo, summerhouse, patio walls and pergola with fragrant climbers. Surround sitting areas with shrubs, perennials and roses noted for their fragrant flowers or foliage. Foliage generally has to be pinched to release its fragrance, a particular joy for people with impaired sight, who appreciate plants with fragrant flowers being close at hand, rather than in the middle of a bed or border.

Create little lawns or paths with aromatic carpeting plants which will scent the air with every step. Use these plants, too, in paved areas, especially around seats and on the patio, planting them in gaps in the paving.

Business people, away all day, need not miss out on flower scents, for a number of plants are at their most fragrant in the evening. Clumps of these at the front gate or door will provide a welcome in complete contrast to the smells of town or city!

SHRUBS

Shrubs with fragrant flowers or foliage can be used liberally around secluded sitting areas, perhaps in association with old and modern roses. Most need sun and well-drained soil.

There are plenty of shrubs with fragrant summer flowers, like the early summer-flowering philadelphus (Mock Orange) (Z5) with powerful orange-blossom scent which is attractive to bees.

Philadelphus, *such as 'Belle Etoile' (a), makes a marvellous companion for roses, such as the new English shrub rose 'Gertrude Jekyll' (b). They give a wonderful combination of fragrances*

(a)

(b)

Philadelphus have white flowers and are marvellous companions for roses: some are quite small shrubs like *P. microphyllus,* (c), while others are medium to large, including the popular 'Belle Etoile' and 'Virginal'.

Buddleias are attractive to butterflies and bees and include several large species like *B. alternifolia* (Z5) with lilac blooms in early summer; *B. globosa* (Z8) with globular orange flowers in early summer; and the ever-popular *B. davidii* varieties (Z5) which produce their long arching spikes, much loved by butterflies, in shades of blue, purple, red or white in late summer.

The medium-size evergreen *Choisya ternata* (Mexican Orange Blossom) (Z7)(c) has white flowers with a powerful orange-blossom fragrance over much of the summer. The small semi-evergreen shrub *Daphne* x *burkwoodii* (Z6)(c) produces its sweetly scented light pink blooms in late spring and early summer.

Many spring-flowering shrubs have fragrant flowers, top of the popularity charts being syringa (Lilac). The most popular, the varieties of *S. vulgaris* (Z4), are unfortunately unsuitable for small gardens due to their large size, although many people unwisely plant them in small plots. More suitable for small gardens is *S. microphylla* 'Superba' (Z4)(c) with pink flowers from late spring to mid-autumn.

Corylopsis pauciflora (Z7)(c) is a small shrub which produces cowslip-scented pale yellow flowers on its bare branches in early spring. It is best grown in lime-free soil. The medium-sized evergreen shrub *Osmanthus delavayi* (Z7)(c) produces a heavy sweet fragrance from its masses of small jasmine-like white flowers.

Flowering in mid- to late spring is *Viburnum carlesii* (Z5)(c), a medium-size shrub with globular heads of white flowers with the fragrance of carnations.

Every garden should have some shrubs with fragrant winter flowers. A very popular winter-flowering shrub is *Chimonanthus praecox* (Z7), of medium size with light yellow flowers on bare twigs. With darker yellow blooms is the variety 'Grandiflorus'. Plant them against a background of dark evergreen shrubs so that the flowers show up.

A similar background is needed for the shrubby Honeysuckles, *Lonicera fragrantissima* and *L.* x *purpusii* (Z6), both medium semi-evergreen shrubs with deliciously fragrant white flowers.

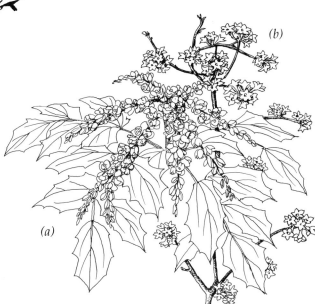

Two favourite fragrant winter-flowering shrubs are Mahonia japonica *(a) with Lily-of-the-valley-scented flowers, and* Viburnum farreri *(b) with an equally delicious perfume*

There are several daphnes (c) which bloom in winter, including the popular *D. mezereum* (Z5), a small upright shrub whose bare branches are wreathed with purplish-red blooms in late winter, and *D. odora* (Z7), a small evergreen species with highly scented purplish-pink flowers in the depths of winter.

Viburnum farreri (V. fragrans) (Z6)(c) grows to quite a large shrub which from late autumn and throughout winter produces deliciously fragrant white blooms from bright pink buds.

Although eventually a medium-size shrub, *Mahonia japonica* (Z6)(c) is fairly slow-growing. It is attractive all year round with its large evergreen leaves, but in the late autumn to early spring it surpasses itself by sporting long chains of yellow Lily-of-the-valley-scented flowers.

Many shrubs have aromatic foliage, most of which have to be pinched to release their fragrance. Rosemary is one of the most popular, and associates particularly well with old-fashioned roses. The flowers attract bees. *Rosmarinus officinalis* (Z7)(c) is the Common Rosemary, a medium evergreen shrub with greyish-green camphorous foliage and blue flowers in summer. There are several good varieties like 'Fastigiatus' (Miss Jessop's Variety) and the dwarf 'Severn Sea'.

Also a good companion for old or modern roses is Lavender with grey-green aromatic foliage and blue flowers in summer which attract swarms of bees. *L. angustifolia* (Old English Lavender) (Z6)(c) is a small shrub with several good varieties like the popular 'Hidcote' and 'Munstead'.

Lippia citriodora (Lemon Plant) (Z8)(c) is a medium-size shrub whose leaves smell strongly of lemon when crushed. It needs a very sheltered position as it is not too hardy. The evergreen *Myrtus communis* (Common Myrtle) (Z8)(c) has strongly aromatic foliage and a profusion of white flowers in summer.

The camphorous leaves of *Laurus nobilis* (Sweet Bay) (Z8)(c) are used for culinary purposes, but this large evergreen shrub is useful in the ornamental garden, too, especially as a background for winter-flowering shrubs.

Although really trees, eucalyptus can be grown as shrubs if they are pruned to near ground level in spring each year. The hardiest is *E. gunnii* (Z8) with silvery-blue young foliage. Also worth trying is *E.*

RIGHT
A bed of Lavender, Rosemary and roses, three plants which are noted for their fragrance, and which combine well together. Fragrant plants need to be grown in sheltered areas if their scent is not to be quickly lost on the wind (THE ROYAL NATIONAL ROSE SOCIETY'S GARDENS, HERTFORDSHIRE)

BELOW RIGHT
Many coastal gardens have superb views and it is important to preserve these, as well as provide shelter for plants. This 'walk' is flanked by aromatic Catmint, which flourishes in maritime gardens (INVEREWE GARDEN, SCOTLAND, NATIONAL TRUST FOR SCOTLAND)

BELOW
Roses can be used in association with suitable shrubs to create some attractive contrasts in shape, colour and texture. The centrepiece of this group is the hybrid musk rose 'Penelope' (a), with deliciously fragrant pale salmon-pink flowers. It contrasts well with the purple-leaved shrub, Cotinus coggygria 'Royal Purple' (b). Further contrast is provided by the dwarf grey-leaved shrub Senecio 'Sunshine' (c) and the silver feathery foliage of Santolina chamaecyparissus (d)

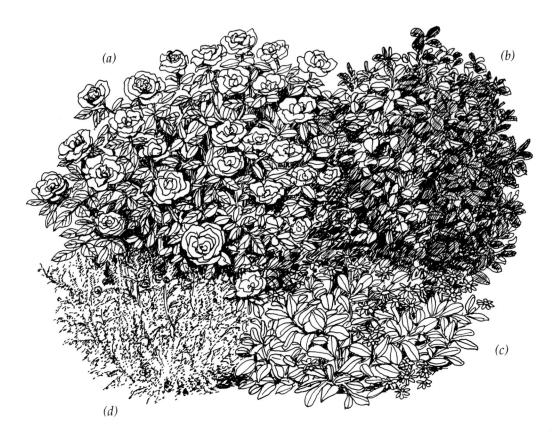

niphophila (Snow Gum) (Z8) with grey-green foliage. Their leaves have a refreshing camphorous fragrance when pinched (c).

Cistus ladanifer (Sun Rose) (Z8)(c) has a powerful resinous fragrance which is particularly noticeable in hot weather. Known as the Gum Cistus, it has white flowers blotched with brown in summer, and is a medium-sized evergreen shrub.

ROSES

One could write a book purely about scented roses as there are so many of them, but here is described a good representative selection of both old and modern kinds. All flower in the summer, and can be grown in containers.

Use roses in association with suitable shrubs and perennials to create some attractive contrasts in shape, colour and texture. Roses need plenty of sun if they are to flower well and should be grown in a fertile, well-drained yet moisture-retentive soil. Most do not need regular pruning; only the large-flowered, cluster-flowered, climbing and rambling roses.

Old and species roses

The Bourbon roses (Z6) are medium-sized shrubs with a repeat-flowering habit. There is a number of very highly fragrant varieties, such as 'Boule de Neige' with cream flowers; 'Honorine de Brabant', striped mauve and purple flowers; 'Louise Odier', deep pink; and 'Mme Isaac Pereire', purple-crimson flowers.

Centifolia roses (cabbage roses) (Z6), with very double globe-shaped blooms, are generally medium-sized shrubs. One of the best-known varieties is the light pink 'Fantin Latour'.

Damask roses (Z5) are noted for their delicious fragrance and are small to medium-sized shrubs. 'Mme Hardy' has white double flowers and 'Omar Khayyam' bears pale pink double blooms.

Rosa eglanteria (Common Sweet Briar) (Z6) is a medium-size shrub whose leaves smell of apples, this being particularly noticeable after rain. During the summer it bears small pale pink flowers, followed by red hips.

Gallica roses (Z6), ranging from smallish to medium-sized shrubs, include some tremendously fragrant varieties, such as 'Belle de Crecy' with pink and mauve flowers, and the dark purple 'Cardinal de Richelieu'.

The flower buds and stalks of moss roses (Z6) are covered with moss-like growths. They are medium-sized shrubs. Some highly fragrant varieties include 'Common Moss' with deep pink cup-shaped blooms and 'White Moss' with white double flowers.

Rosa primula (the Incense Rose) (Z7) is a medium-sized shrub which produces small single yellow blooms in the spring. The popular name refers to the foliage which has the fragrance of incense.

Old-fashioned climbing roses (Z6) which have good fragrance include 'Cécile Brunner' with very small pale pink flowers; 'Gloire de Dijon' (yellow, tinted with pink, repeat-flowering); 'Mme Alfred Carrière' (small white blooms, tinted pink, repeat-flowering); 'Mme Grégoire Staechelin' (large light pink blooms); and 'Zéphirine Drouhin' (a thornless variety with bright reddish-pink blooms, repeat-flowering).

These climbers should be pruned annually in early spring by reducing lateral shoots to within one to three growth buds.

Modern roses

The large-flowered roses, which used to be known as hybrid teas (Z6), are very formal, with large

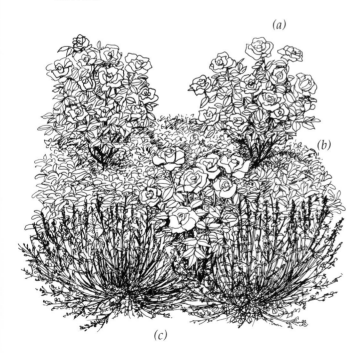

Large-flowered roses (a) are best suited to mass planting in formal rose beds, underplanted with dwarf perennials such as Stachys lanata *'Silver Carpet' (b), with woolly silver-grey leaves, and nepeta or Catmint (c), with greyish foliage and blue flowers in summer*

perfectly formed flowers produced in several flushes throughout the summer. The average height of these bush roses is 90cm (3ft), although some will make medium-sized plants and a few are shorter. They are, perhaps, best suited to mass planting in formal rose beds, underplanted with dwarf perennials such as nepeta, aubrieta, *Stachys lanata* 'Silver Carpet', ajuga and dwarf ground-cover campanulas. Underplant, too, with dwarf spring-flowering bulbs like muscari, chionodoxa, scilla and bulbous irises. Underplanting creates colour and interest when the roses are out of flower.

The large-flowered roses have to be pruned annually in early spring by cutting back all strong stems by half to two-thirds of their length, and shortening weaker ones to 5-8cm (2-3in). This hard pruning results in good-quality flowers.

Many large-flowered varieties unfortunately possess little scent, so one has to choose with care if fragrance is top priority. Some highly fragrant varieties include 'Alec's Red' with deep red blooms; the coral-salmon 'Blessings', 'Fragrant Cloud' with coral-scarlet flowers which have a very heavy fragrance; the salmon-pink 'Fragrant Hour'; 'Keepsake' with cherry pink blooms; peach-coloured 'Paul Shirville'; rose-pink 'Prima Ballerina'; deep velvety crimson 'Royal William'; and pink and apricot 'Woods of Windsor'.

Cluster-flowered roses (Z6) are also rather formal and best grown in the same way as large-flowered varieties. These are also bush roses, and average height is 90-120cm (3-4ft). The blooms are carried in large clusters, and several flushes are produced throughout the summer. The cluster-flowered roses also need annual pruning in early spring, by cutting back by one-third to half their length all strong stems; weaker stems are reduced by two-thirds to encourage stronger growth.

Once again varieties have to be chosen with care for many have little or no fragrance. Those recommended for strong fragrance include 'Ann Aberconway' (orange-yellow); 'Arthur Bell' (brilliant yellow); 'Elizabeth of Glamis' (salmon and pink); 'Isis' (white, tinted pink); 'Korresia' (deep yellow); 'Margaret Merril' (white, tinted pink); 'Matangi' (orange-red); 'Moon Maiden' (cream-yellow); 'Mountbatten' (pure yellow); 'Scented Air' (salmon-pink); 'Shocking Blue' (dark magenta flushed with mauve); 'Southampton' (pale orange); and 'Young Venturer' (orange-yellow).

An arbour (a shady recess or bower) where one can sit is easily constructed from timber trellis panels. This makes an ideal support for fragrant climbing plants, such as Jasminum officinale, *the Common White Jasmine. Aromatic carpeting plants, like thymes, can be grown in gaps in the paving in front of the arbour*

CLIMBERS

Many of the modern climbing roses (Z6) are repeat-flowering: that is, they produce several flushes of blooms throughout the summer. It is sensible to choose these rather than varieties which produce only one crop of blooms in the summer. The blooms are large, often resembling those of large-flowered and cluster-flowered roses. Annual pruning is needed in early spring, which simply involves cutting back all lateral or side shoots to within one to three growth buds of their base.

Varieties with good fragrance include 'Compassion' (salmon and orange); 'Dreaming Spires' (brilliant deep yellow); 'Elizabeth Heather Grierson' (pink); 'Kathleen Harrop' (palest pink); 'Malaga' (deep bright pink); 'Schoolgirl' (apricot, tinted pink); 'Souvenir de C. Denoyel' (deep crimson); and 'Summer Wine' (coral-pink single flowers with conspicuous red stamens).

The spidery flowers of hamamelis or Witch Hazel, which make such a welcome display in the winter, are often fragrant. This is an excellent if slow-growing shrub for the dappled shade of the woodland garden, although it is equally at home in a shrub or mixed border (HILLIER ARBORETUM, AMPFIELD, HAMPSHIRE)

RIGHT

In this informal rose garden, old-fashioned roses are combined with other plants. Many of the old-fashioned roses have a powerful perfume, but one of their drawbacks is that so many of them have only one flush of flowers during the summer
(GARDEN IN HARTLEY WINTNEY, BERKSHIRE)

MODERN SHRUB ROSES

The modern repeat-flowering shrub roses (Z6), which produce several flushes of blooms throughout summer, are ideal for mixed and shrub borders and need no regular pruning. Most are medium-sized shrubs. Few of them are fragrant, but those which can be recommended for their scent include 'Cardinal Hume' with dark purple flowers; 'Golden Wings', with large single yellow blooms and conspicuous orange stamens; 'Lavender Lassie', with big clusters of lavender-pink flowers; and 'Magenta', with double magenta-mauve flowers.

The new English roses have caused something of a sensation recently. They have been produced by crossing old shrub roses with modern varieties, and have some of the desirable characteristics of the old varieties – fully double flowers and tremendous fragrance – and of the modern roses – a wide range of colours and a long season of colour. They make small to medium-sized bushes, depending on variety. Varieties include 'Gertrude Jekyll' with very large deep pink rosette-like flowers; 'Graham Thomas', with cup-shaped double blooms in deep golden-yellow; 'Heritage', with fully double cup-shaped blooms in pure pale pink; 'Mary Rose', with very double blooms in deep pink; and 'William Shakespeare' with dark crimson rosette-like flowers which turn to deep purple as they age.

HYBRID MUSK ROSES

These modern repeat-flowering shrub roses (Z6) were raised at the beginning of this century. With exquisite fragrance, the blooms are carried on medium-sized bushes which are suitable for informal planting with other shrubs and perennials.

Some well-known varieties include 'Buff Beauty' (shades of buff-yellow and orange); 'Cornelia' (pink blooms tinted with orange); 'Felicia' (blush-pink); 'Moonlight' (light creamy-white with conspicuous deep gold stamens); 'Penelope' (pale salmon-pink); and 'Prosperity' (white double flowers).

CLIMBERS

Climbing plants should be grown in every garden to make the most of otherwise wasted vertical space. Grow them on patio walls or over a patio pergola in order to savour their fragrance while relaxing.

Climbers can be grown in other sitting areas, too,

*Try combining climbing roses, such as
'Compassion' (a), with* Jasminum officinale,
*the Common White Jasmine (b), and
clematis. The clematis shown here
is the fragrant white* C. flammula *(c)*

(c)

(a)

(b)

*A climber can be grown over a gazebo,
an ornamental building used as
a vantage point from where one can sit
and look out over the garden.
A climbing rose is most suitable,
as it will not completely smother the building!*

such as over an arbour (a shady recess or bower). An attractive garden feature is an arbour covering and partially enclosing a garden seat. There are various ways of constructing this, but perhaps the easiest is to use timber trellis panels, forming them into a box-shaped structure over the seat but open at the front. This makes an ideal support for fragrant climbing plants. The 'floor' of the arbour should ideally be paved so that it is dry and free from mud in wet weather. Carpeting aromatic plants could be grown in gaps in the paving in front of the arbour (do not grow them inside as it would be too shady).

Climbers can also be grown over a gazebo. This is an ornamental building used as a vantage point where one can sit and look out over the garden. It can be open or partially open (not enclosed like a summerhouse) and should ideally have a roof so that it can be used in wet weather. It is possible to buy gazebos from specialist garden-building suppliers. How about a circular structure with a domed roof, in wrought iron? Painted white it would make a marvellous focal point in the garden and a superb support for climbing plants.

Summerhouses are very popular today, as they were as early as the fifteenth century, making a pleasant and comfortable retreat from the house where one can sit and admire the garden. Modern summerhouses are usually made from western red cedar, or similar timber. It is a good idea to pave an area in front of the summerhouse so that you can sit outside in clement weather. Leave gaps in the paving and plant aromatic carpeting plants in them. Fragrant climbing plants can be grown over the summerhouse.

Among the most popular fragrant climbers are the loniceras or Honeysuckles (c) which flower in the summer. *L. periclymenum* (Z5) has some good varieties like 'Belgica' (early Dutch Honeysuckle) and 'Serotina' (late Dutch Honeysuckle), with reddish-purple-flushed flowers. *L. x americana* (Z5) is very vigorous, with white blooms which turn deep yellow. *L. x heckrottii* (Z4) has a semi-climbing habit and purple-flushed yellow blooms. *L. caprifolium* (Perfoliate Honeysuckle) (Z6) is vigorous and produces cream-white blooms. Try to shade the root area of Honeysuckles and ensure their tops are in the sun.

Clematis (c) like these conditions, too. There are several fragrant species including *C. flammula* (Z5) with small white blooms in summer; *C. montana*

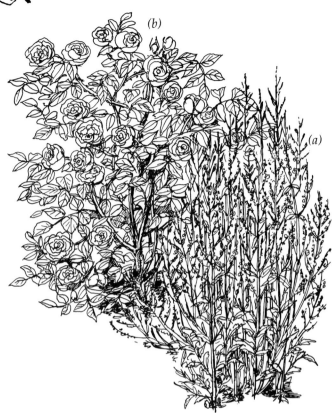

A herbaceous perennial which makes an excellent companion for shrub roses, contrasting well in shape, colour and texture, is Perovskia atriplicifolia *'Blue Spire' (a) with deep blue flowers and grey-green foliage. Here it has been combined with the bourbon rose 'Mme Isaac Pereire' (b) with purple-crimson highly fragrant flowers*

'Alexander' (Z5), with cream flowers in late spring and early summer; and *C. rehderana* with pendulous, bell-like, yellow blooms in late summer and autumn.

Jasminum officinale (Common White Jasmine) (Z6)(c) is a vigorous deciduous climber with a profusion of white flowers from early summer to autumn. It is suitable for a shady spot.

Although not a climber, *Cytisus battandieri* (Z7)(c) makes a good wall shrub and produces spikes of yellow blooms which have the fragrance of pineapples in summer. It needs plenty of sun.

Climbing roses should be considered, too. Good fragrant varieties have been described under Roses (p.112). Try combining them with clematis and White Jasmine.

A superb combination of fragrant plants. *Philadelphus* or *Mock Orange*, a shrub with white flowers which appear in early summer, grey *Catmint* with blue flowers, and pink and white shrub roses, backed by a purple-leaved *cotinus* or *Smoke Bush*
(*VALE END, SURREY*)

Climbing roses should not be forgotten, as many of them provide fragrance, including the old yet still popular 'Mme Alfred Carrière'. The large double globular flowers appear in the summer, even if the plant is grown against a shady wall
(*LOWER BROOK HOUSE, SHROPSHIRE*)

A summerhouse makes a pleasant and comfortable retreat from the house and can be surrounded by fragrant plants. The summerhouse itself forms an ideal support for scented climbing plants
(*LOWER BROOK HOUSE, SHROPSHIRE*)

HARDY PERENNIALS

Hardy perennials with fragrant flowers, or foliage which emits scent when pinched, should be included with shrubs and other plants around secluded sitting areas. Most need sunny well-drained conditions.

Those perennials which have to be pinched to release their foliage scent include *Calamintha nepetoides*, an upright moderately hardy perennial with strongly aromatic leaves. Lilac or white flowers are produced in late summer and autumn.

Helichrysum angustifolium (Curry Plant) (Z7)(c) is excellent for combining with roses, as its silvery-grey foliage contrasts well with them. It is highly aromatic, with the smell of curry. A small bushy evergreen plant, it produces heads of small yellow flowers in summer.

With foliage smelling strongly of lemons when pinched, *Melissa officinalis* (Lemon Balm)(c) is a very hardy small upright herbaceous plant with whorls of tiny white flowers in late summer.

Nepeta or Catmint (c) with greyish-green highly aromatic foliage is excellent for underplanting roses. The one usually grown is *Nepeta* x *faassenii* (Z4), a low bushy plant with spikes of light blue flowers throughout summer.

A herbaceous perennial which makes an excellent companion for shrub roses, contrasting well in shape, texture and colour, is *Perovskia atriplicifolia* (Z7). Up to 1.5m (5ft) high, it produces spikes of deep blue flowers in late summer and early autumn. The grey-green foliage is strongly aromatic. 'Blue Spire', with deep blue flowers, is a good variety.

Perennials with fragrant flowers include the ever-popular *Convallaria majalis* (Lily-of-the-valley) (Z3). Of ground-covering habit, this spring-flowering plant has small white bell-shaped blooms which are very sweetly scented. There are several varieties, such as the double-flowered 'Plena' and the pink 'Rosea'. They are best grown in partial shade and moisture-retentive humus-rich soil.

Dianthus (Pinks and Carnations)(c) are generally noted for fragrance, although by no means all have this virtue and indeed many modern varieties of border pinks lack fragrance. Some dianthus species which have scented flowers include *D. arenarius* (Z5) with white blooms in summer and *D. caesius* (Cheddar Pink) (Z5) with pink blooms in early to mid-summer. Well-scented border Carnations (Z5) which bloom in mid-summer include 'Imperial

Clove' (carmine flowers); 'Lavender Clove' (lavender-coloured); 'Merlin Clove' (white and red); 'Perfect Clove' (rich deep crimson); and 'Robin Thain' (white and deep red).

FRAGRANT WALKS

Little lawns and even paths can be created with aromatic carpeting plants, especially Chamomile, Thymes and Mints, which will give off scent with every step. If these lawns or paths are to receive very heavy use it would be a good idea to run stepping stones through them, for although the plants mentioned will tolerate a reasonable amount of walking on, they are not as tough as lawn grasses.

The Chamomile to use for a lawn or path is the non-flowering variety of *Anthemis nobilis* called 'Treneague' (Z6). This forms a dark green springy lawn which is particularly fragrant after a shower of rain. It has creeping stems which root into the ground as they grow. It is best grown in full sun and light, very well-drained soil; avoid shade and wet soils. To create a Chamomile lawn or path, young plants should be planted 15cm (6in) apart each way in the spring, in well-cultivated completely weed-free ground. Chamomile does not need regular mowing like grass, but should be lightly trimmed with shears or mower in late summer to keep it neat.

Carpeting Thymes can be used in the same way and require identical growing conditions. *Thymus serpyllum* (Z5) is a prostrate carpeting species with tiny greyish-green leaves and small flowers in summer. There are several varieties like crimson 'Coccineus', pink 'Annie Hall', white 'Albus' and mauve 'Lanuginosus' with woolly grey foliage. *T. herba-barona* (Caraway Thyme) (Z6) is a carpeting species with small deep green leaves which have the fragrance of caraway and light mauve flowers in early summer. Trim the Thymes lightly after flowering to remove dead blooms and to maintain a neat habit of growth.

Carpeting Mints (Z6) which can be used for making lawns or paths include *Mentha pulegium* (Pennyroyal), with tiny peppermint-scented leaves and mauve flowers in summer. *Mentha requienii* also has peppermint-scented leaves and light purple flowers in summer. The Mints are best grown in moisture-retentive soil, in sun or partial shade. *M. requienii* prefers partial shade. Plant in the same way as Chamomile.

Chamomile, Thymes and Mints can also be used

for planting in gaps in paving around sitting areas, again to provide fragrance when they are trodden on.

Fragrant seats

If you have a bank in the garden consider having a wooden seat recessed into it and clothing the bank all around it with Chamomile, Thymes or Mints. Alternatively, instead of having timber to sit on, plant the seat with fragrant carpeting plants so that they give off fragrance when you sit down. The front of such a seat would need to be reinforced, say with timber, bricks or ornamental concrete walling blocks, as shown here.

EVENING SCENT

For those who are away all day, plants which give off their fragrance in the evening are especially welcome. Plant generous groups around sitting areas and alongside the front gate or door where they will provide a fragrant homecoming.

Suitable plants include *Hesperis matronalis* (Sweet Rocket) (Z3)(c) a short-lived herbaceous perennial which in early summer produces spikes of small four-petalled flowers in white, or shades of purple or mauve. It grows to about 90cm (3ft). Plant it in a sunny spot with light well-drained yet moisture-retentive soil. Sweet Rocket generally self-sows freely, but can be raised by sowing seeds outdoors in spring; or roots can be divided in the autumn.

Matthiola bicornis (Night-scented Stock) (c) is a hardy annual, seeds of which are sown outdoors in mid-spring where the plants are to flower. Growing to about 30cm (1ft) in height, Night-scented Stock produces spikes of mauve four-petalled flowers in summer.

Nicotiana (Ornamental Tobacco) (c) is grown as a half-hardy annual for summer display. Varieties of *N. alata* and *N. x sanderae* are widely grown and most open their fragrant flowers in the evening. The strain 'Evening Fragrance' is noted particularly for

A wooden seat can be recessed into a bank and surrounded by fragrant Chamomile. Even the part you sit on has been planted with Chamomile, so fragrance is given off when you sit down

this habit; its flowers come in shades of pink, rose, red, mauve, purple and white, and it reaches a height of about 90cm (3ft). Sow seeds of nicotiana in a heated greenhouse during early spring and plant out when danger of frost is over, choosing a sunny spot with fertile well-drained soil.

Oenothera (Evening Primrose) species often open their flowers in the evening and some are fragrant, particularly *O. trichocalyx* (Z5)(c), a biennial, or perennial surviving for several years, with white deliciously scented flowers in early summer. Raise plants by sowing seeds under glass in mid-spring and plant out young plants in a sunny well-drained spot. They grow to about 45cm (18in).

The scent of Border Phloxes, varieties of *P. paniculata* (Z4), is good in the evening. They are tall plants, 90-120cm (3-4ft) in height, and come in a very wide range of colours. They are best grown in

One is assured of fragrance when sitting in this secluded corner, as the seat is set in a Chamomile lawn. Chamomile is particularly fragrant after a shower of rain, and walking on it also releases scent. It is best grown in full sun and light, very well-drained soil (SURREY END COTTAGE, SURREY)

Some bulbs have fragrant flowers, including Acidanthera bicolor murielae. The blooms appear in late summer and early autumn. This bulb is not too hardy, but can be grown outside all the year round in areas which do not have severe winters

partial shade and fertile, moisture-retentive, humus-rich soil, and bloom in mid- to late summer.

The creamy-white flowers of *Reseda odorata* (Mignonette) (c) are well-scented in the evening. This is a hardy annual, 30-60cm (1-2ft) in height, which blooms throughout summer. Sow seeds outdoors in early to mid-spring, where the plants are to flower, choosing a sunny spot with fertile well-drained soil. They flourish in alkaline soils.

Wildlife

The current awareness of the importance of conserving our natural heritage is particularly strong among gardeners, who also have the facilities for putting conservation into practice.

Sheltered, secluded, densely planted gardens are havens for a variety of wildlife including birds, insects, small mammals and amphibians, especially if a good range of wild flowers is grown. Dense natural hedges will encourage birds to nest and roost; many wild flowers will attract butterflies, bees and other insects; and a natural pond will be a home and meeting place for all kinds of creatures.

You do not need a large garden in order to create suitable habitats for wildlife: many gardeners have several mini-habitats in pocket-handkerchief-size plots. It is a case of deciding that you definitely want to grow wild flowers and attract wildlife, then incorporating the necessary features into the garden, blending them in with the more usual things. For instance, a small pond does not take up much space; and a mini wild-flower meadow could be an extension of the lawn. Instead of having a formal clipped hedge for privacy and shelter, plant a natural or 'country' hedge instead, which will attract far more in the way of wildlife.

WETLAND HABITAT

This is the conservationist's term for a pond. It is possibly the most exciting and rewarding wildlife habitat as it attracts frogs, newts, dragonflies, damselflies, toads and herons (these will be trying to catch fish for their breakfast, so beware!). Mammals like hedgehogs and foxes may use a pond for drinking, even in urban areas, and birds will be attracted for the same purpose.

A pond should be sited in an open sunny position to ensure water plants flourish, and there should be plenty of these.

Make the pond as natural-looking as possible, ideally slightly sunken with grass right up to the edge so that wildlife can easily reach the water. Today natural-looking ponds are easily constructed simply by lining a suitably shaped excavation with black butyl-rubber pool liner. The excavation should first be lined with soft sand or proprietary underlay to prevent stones from puncturing the liner. The edges, which should overlap the sides of the pond, can be hidden and secured with turves. Make sure the pond is deep enough; a minimum depth is 45cm (18in). The sides should slope slightly inwards for stability and it is a good idea to form shelves around the sides on which you can grow marginal aquatics which need shallow water.

The pond should be well stocked with aquatics, especially submerged oxygenators or 'water weeds' like *Lagarosiphon major* (Common Fish Weed), *Myriophyllum* species (Milfoils) and *Hottonia palustris* (Water Violet). These help to keep the water clear.

A small Waterlily will help to shade the pool from excessive sun and should be grown in the deeper water. About one-third of the water surface can be covered with lily 'pads'.

In the shallow water around the edge of the pool grow plenty of marginal or marsh plants like *Iris pseudacorus* (Yellow Flag Iris) (Z5) which blooms in late spring and summer. The Reed-maces (also known as Bulrushes) (Z5) are almost essential marginal plants. *Typha angustifolia* is popularly known as the Lesser Bulrush or Reed-mace and is the best choice for a small pool. Needing a large pool or lake is *T. latifolia*, the Great Reed-mace or False Bulrush. Both produce long fat sausage-like brown flower spikes.

Rushes or juncus can be included, too. There are several species, but the Common Rush is *Juncus effusus* (Z5) with deep green stems. Curious and amusing is its variety *spiralis* with twisted stems, like a corkscrew.

The marginal plants and Waterlilies can be planted in special plastic aquatic baskets using a heavy loamy soil. Submerged kinds are simply dropped into the water.

In the moist soil around the edge of the pond plant moisture-loving plants like the beautiful *Caltha palustris* (Marsh Marigold) (Z4) which produces golden blooms in spring. *Filipendula ulmaria* (Meadowsweet) (Z4) has feathery heads of cream flowers in summer and the seeds which follow will be relished by birds. Butterflies and moths will be attracted to the pink summer flowers of *Lychnis flos-cuculi* (Ragged Robin) (Z2) and to the spikes of red-purple summer flowers of *Lythrum salicaria* (Purple Loosestrife) (Z3). Some moth caterpillars feed on the leaves of the latter.

Ranunculus lingua (Greater Spearwort) (Z2) is a moisture-loving buttercup with large yellow flowers in summer. With similar but globe-shaped blooms in summer is *Trollius europaeus* (Globeflower) (Z2). Bearing trusses of attractive pink flowers in summer is *Eupatorium cannabinum* (Hemp Agrimony) (Z6). Also favouring moist ground is *Succisa pratensis* (Devilsbit Scabious) (Z3) with rounded heads of blue-purple or pink flowers from early summer onwards.

A pond for wildlife should be as natural-looking as possible with grass right up to the edge. This is most easily achieved by lining a suitably shaped excavation with black butyl-rubber pool liner. Use plenty of oxygenating and marginal plants, and a Waterlily or two. If desired, plants can be set in a layer of heavy soil placed in the bottom of the pool

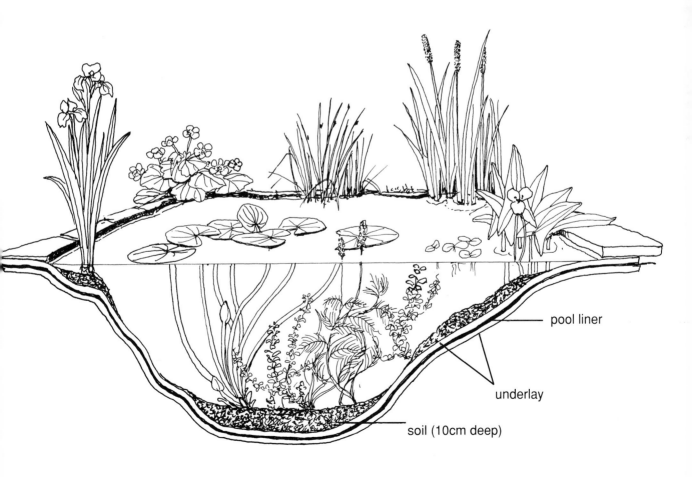

pool liner

underlay

soil (10cm deep)

A NATURAL HEDGE

A natural hedge is a marvellous wildlife habitat as it encourages birds to nest and roost. It provides food for birds, too, in the form of berries and fruits. As with all hedges it creates sheltered areas in the garden which are more likely to encourage butter-flies than exposed windy gardens. A natural hedge could be used to surround a wildlife area, or as a boundary for all or part of the garden. Don't be afraid to plant a natural hedge in a town or subur-ban garden (even though all your neighbours may have neatly trimmed privet hedges) for it will not look out of place.

Natural hedges are grown informally – in other words, should not be trimmed hard – although some judicious trimming will be needed to keep them reasonably tidy.

Grow a mixture of shrubs and trees and encour-age some wild climbing plants to scramble through the hedge. The shrubs can be spaced about 45cm (18in) apart in a row to form the hedge.

Crataegus monogyna (Hawthorn) (Z5), although really a tree, can be grown as a hedge by topping it at the required height to keep it bushy. It has white

fragrant flowers in spring followed by red berries (food for birds) in autumn and it is deciduous. *Ilex aquifolium* (Common Holly) (Z7) is evergreen and produces red berries in autumn and winter if male and female plants are grown together. *Rosa canina* (Dog Rose) (Z4) is very prickly and has pink flowers in summer followed by red fruits.

Sambucus nigra (Elder) (Z6) is worth including; it is a deciduous shrub with scented cream blooms in early summer followed by black berries. There are two viburnums worth including in the natural hedge. One is *Viburnum lantana* (Wayfaring Tree) (Z3) which has cream flowers in early summer followed by red berries and red autumn leaf colour. The other is *V. opulus* (Guelder Rose) (Z3) whose foliage takes on brilliant tints in autumn. It has white blooms in early summer followed by clusters of red berries.

A small tree could be included in the hedge if space permits. A good food tree for birds is *Sorbus aucuparia* (Mountain Ash, Rowan) (Z2), which pro-duces large clusters of bright red berries in the autumn. These are soon devoured! Pruning will maintain the Mountain Ash as a shrub, but then there will be few if any berries.

LEFT
*This superb example of a natural looking, man-made pond is designed to attract wildlife such as frogs, newts, dragonflies, birds and mammals. The surrounds are well-furnished with wild plants which will attract further creatures (*CHRIS BAINES' WILDLIFE GARDEN*)*

RIGHT
Many wild orchids, such as this Spotted Orchid, attract insects of various kinds, so plant a good selection of native species in areas of the garden devoted to wildlife

For scrambling through the hedge plant some climbers: *Clematis vitalba* (Traveller's Joy) (Z6) with white flowers in summer followed by silky seed heads; *Lonicera periclymenum* (Wild Honeysuckle) (Z5) with fragrant cream red-tinted blooms in summer followed by red berries; and *Rubus fruticosus* (Bramble), a prickly semi-evergreen scrambler producing blackberries in late summer and autumn.

Along the bottom of the hedge sow suitable wild-flower seeds. Collections for hedgerows are available from wild-flower seedsmen.

WOODLAND

A natural woodland habitat is only possible if you are one of those fortunate gardeners with an area of woodland in the garden. To create a wildlife habitat leave all or part of it completely natural, allowing fallen leaves and tree branches to remain, making a home for all kinds of insects and other creatures.

Wild flowers which enjoy the dappled shade of the woodland, and whose flowers attract insects, can be planted in bold drifts or groups. Seeds of these are available from wild-flower specialists, and all are (Z3).

Drifts of Bluebells *(Endymion nonscriptus)* make a stunning display in spring and early summer. Closely following these comes *Digitalis purpurea* (Foxglove) with tall spikes of pink, purplish or white flowers. *Primula vulgaris* (Primrose) is an almost essential spring-flowering wild flower, and another that should be in every woodland is *Viola odorata* (Sweet Violet) with violet-blue flowers in spring. *Aquilegia vulgaris* (Columbine) produces blue or pink flowers in early summer. *Symphytum officinale* (Common Comfrey) is a good woodland plant with white, blue or pink flowers throughout summer. Bright rose-pink flowers are produced over the same period by *Silene dioica* (Red Campion).

The biennial *Dipsacus fullonum* (Wild Teasel) attracts varied wildlife when in flower, including the common blue and small copper butterflies and bumblebees. The seeds are relished by goldfinches.

THE CORNFIELD

An open sunny yet sheltered position with infertile soil makes an ideal site for a cornfield. This is not as ambitious as it sounds for it is simply an area sown with colourful annual wild flowers which were once a common sight in cornfields. Many of the wild flowers used attract butterflies, bees, hoverflies and other insects.

To create a cornfield the ground should be dug, firmed and raked down to a fine tilth suitable for sowing seeds. The seeds are sown in the spring. As the plants should subsequently self-sow there should be no need for further sowings.

Highly colourful annual wild flowers (Z3), which bloom in the summer, include *Papaver rhoeas* (Field Poppy) with deep scarlet poppy flowers. With rounded reddish-purple flowers is *Agrostemma githago* (Corn Cockle) while much-loved by bees and butterflies is *Centaurea cyanus* (Cornflower) with heads of blue flowers. The latter contrasts particularly well with corn marigolds and field poppies.

Butterflies are also very fond of *Chrysanthemum segetum* (Corn Marigold) with bright yellow daisy-like flowers, and *Viola tricolor* (Heartsease) with yellow and purple flowers from spring to autumn. *Tripleurospermum maritimum* (Scentless Mayweed) contrasts well with Field Poppies as it bears numerous small white daisy-like flowers. Last but not least consider *Sinapsis arvensis* (Charlock), a cabbage relation with heads of yellow flowers.

Stinging-nettle patch

Somewhere in the garden in full sun, perhaps on the edge of the cornfield or alongside the hedge, have a patch of Stinging Nettles *(Urtica dioica)* (Z4) to attract butterflies like the peacock, red admiral, painted lady, comma and small tortoiseshell. These lay their eggs on Stinging Nettles and the caterpillars feed on the leaves.

Nettles are extremely vigorous and spreading, particularly on rich soil which they prefer. In good conditions plants can grow up to 1.2m (4ft) high. To

Marginal plants and Waterlilies can be planted in special plastic aquatic baskets, using heavy loamy soil, as an alternative to having a layer of soil in the bottom of the pool

prevent the nettles from spreading, dig a trench all round the site, about 45cm (18in) deep; line this with thick polythene sheeting, the top of which should be at soil level. Then refill the trench with soil.

MEADOWLAND

Meadowland is a more ambitious undertaking than a cornfield, but it is undoubtedly one of the most attractive wildlife habitats. It consists of an area of long grass with wild flowers growing in it. These attract butterflies like the common blue, meadow brown, orange-tip, small copper and skippers; as well as other insects like bees, hoverflies and grasshoppers.

It is best to buy a properly balanced grass-seed and wild-flower mixture from a specialist seedsman, which should suit the soil type and climate. The following are suitable for cool temperate climates.

A grass-seed and wild-flower mixture for acid or lime-free soils might contain *Lotus corniculatus* (Bird's-foot Trefoil), a creeping plant with masses of yellow pea-like flowers which attract the common blue butterfly; and *Campanula rotundifolia* (Harebell) with nodding blue bell-like flowers.

A mixture for limy or alkaline soils will contain a good range of 'butterfly plants' like *Leucanthemum vulgare* (Ox-eye Daisy) with white daisy-like flowers; *Cardamine pratensis* (Lady's Smock) with heads of lilac flowers, attracting such butterflies as orange-tip and green-veined white; *Ranunculus acris* (Meadow Buttercup) with bright yellow flowers; *Achillea millefolium* (Yarrow) with flat heads of white flowers; *Ononis repens* (Common Restharrow), whose pink pea-shaped flowers attract the common blue butterfly; *Bellis perennis* (Daisy) with white daisy flowers (a common weed in lawns); *Centaurea scabiosa* (Greater Knapweed) with purple thistle-like flowers whose seeds provide food for birds; *Trifolium repens* (Wild White Clover), a creeping plant with white blooms much loved by bees (also a common weed in lawns); *Knautia arvensis* (Field Scabious), whose blue or lilac flowers attract butterflies and bees in profusion; *Leontodon hispidus* (Greater Hawkbit) with yellow dandelion-like flowers, a food plant for caterpillars; and *Hieracium pilosella* (Mouse-ear Hawkweed), also with yellow dandelion-like flowers whose leaves are relished by various caterpillars.

A meadow on alkaline soil should also contain *Primula veris* (Cowslip) with yellow blooms in spring; and *Prunella vulgaris* (Self-heal), a creeping plant with spikes of violet flowers.

Some of the grasses used in mixtures have attractive flowers, including *Briza media* (Quaking Grass), *Koeleria gracilis* (Crested Hair-grass) and *Hordeum secalinum* (Meadow Barley).

The site for meadowland should be open and sunny, but well sheltered from wind to ensure butterflies and other insects visit it. The soil should be infertile (an unusual recommendation in gardening) as this ensures the wild flowers have less competition from the grasses.

It is essential that you start from scratch, because you will never achieve success by sowing wild flowers in an established lawn. For a start, sowing would prove difficult; then the lawn grasses would be much too vigorous for the well-being of the wild flowers, which would simply be smothered out by the grasses.

If you want to turn existing lawn into a wild-flower meadow, first kill off the grass by treating it with weedkiller such as glyphosate. On bare land use a weedkiller again to kill off weeds. The site should then be thoroughly dug, well firmed and raked down to a fine tilth to create a seed bed for sowing.

The optimum sowing time is early autumn, the second best being early to mid-spring. It is absolutely vital to sow the mixture thinly – 25g per m^2 (¾oz per sq yd). If you sow thickly there will be too many grasses in the area which will then compete with the wild flowers.

The established meadow should be mown in mid-summer, by which time the wild flowers will be over, and again in early autumn. The height of cut should be 5cm (2in) and hay must be raked off.

WHERE TO BUY

A vast range of wild-flower seeds is available from specialist seedsmen, and some of the more popular kinds from general seedsmen. They can be bought as individual species or as mixtures for special purposes (including grass and wild-flower mixtures). Young plants of the most popular kinds are often available from garden centres or nurserymen. On no account obtain plants or seeds from the countryside.

A wild-flower meadow in the garden situation. It is important to create such a meadow with a properly balanced grass-seed and wild-flower mixture. Many of the grasses themselves have attractive flowers
(LOWER BROOK HOUSE, SHROPSHIRE)

Creating a wild-flower meadow is rather ambitious, but it is considered one of the most attractive wildlife habitats. This is an extensive natural meadow, including Ox-eye Daisies, but the scheme can be scaled down for gardens
(NORTH MEADOW, CRICKLADE, WILTSHIRE)

Scabious, both wild species and cultivated varieties, attract various kinds of insects including butterflies and moths. Here the burnet moth is drinking nectar from a cultivated Scabious

Garden Rooms

Garden rooms or conservatories were popular with the Victorians, then suffered a period of neglect and are now more popular than ever before. There can be no more sheltered area for plants than a garden room.

SITING THE GARDEN ROOM
The garden room is generally erected on one of the house walls, with access from one of the rooms. It is even possible to have a conservatory in a roof garden, provided this is structurally feasible. Here, the

A conservatory can be elevated to the first-floor level of a house, but it would have to be designed and supplied by one of the conservatory specialists. (This one was supplied by the UK company, Machin Designs)

services of an architect or structural engineer would have to be employed. A conservatory can also be elevated to the first-floor level of a house, but it would have to be designed and supplied by one of the conservatory specialists.

Ideally a garden room should be sited in a sunny position so that the structure is heated, for at least part of the time, by the sun, so reducing heating bills. The majority of conservatory plants need some sun, although they should be shaded from really strong sunshine to prevent leaf and flower scorch.

If there is no option but to site a garden room on a shady or partially shaded wall then shade-loving plants will have to be grown. Fortunately there is quite a reasonable range of these, such as camellias, primulas, hedera, impatiens, bromeliads, hydrangeas, ferns and foliage begonias.

A garden room on a shady wall will be more expensive to heat due to lack of natural warmth,

When contemplating a garden room liaise with your local planning department, for although planning permission is not needed for conservatories (except when they are to be erected against listed buildings), they do need approval under the building regulations as they must conform to standard specifications. The company supplying the conservatory will provide all necessary plans and specifications of the building. Contact your local planning department to find out what action you need to take.

WAYS OF DISPLAYING PLANTS
A garden room, apart from providing living space for its owner, is very much a place for displaying plants attractively. There are many ways of achieving this.

Beds and borders

A traditional way of displaying conservatory plants is to grow them in soil beds or borders, particularly the larger and permanent kinds such as shrubs and climbers. A border could be constructed along one side of the building, or along the back wall. Alternatively, space permitting, a bed could be sited in the centre so that plants are viewed from all sides.

Ground-level beds should be made when constructing the base or floor of the conservatory, as these areas are not concreted. Raised beds or borders can be constructed on the concrete base. They should be built to a height of 45cm (18in), but not against the walls of the structure as this can cause problems from rising damp.

The beds or borders can be built up from various materials, such as bricks, ornamental concrete walling blocks or even sections of tree trunk if you want a more natural, informal effect. They should be filled with good-quality topsoil such as a light to medium loam.

Ornamental tubs

Alternatively, large plants like shrubs and climbers can be grown in ornamental tubs. The traditional-style square wooden tubs painted white, are worth considering, but tubs are also available in terracotta and reconstituted stone, in both classical and modern styles. Make sure they are large enough for the plants – those with a diameter and depth of 45cm (18in) and upwards are recommended.

ABOVE RIGHT

A conservatory bed or border can be built up with logs or sections of tree trunk if a natural, informal effect is required. There are many exciting subjects for planting in the intermediate-temperature conservatory, such as Strelitzia reginae *(a),* Brunfelsia calycina *(b) and* Hibiscus rosa-sinensis *(c)*

RIGHT

A moss pole *makes an attractive support for climbers which produce aerial roots from their stems, such as* Monstera deliciosa, *the Swiss Cheese Plant. It is easily made at home from a broom handle, wire netting and sphagnum moss. The plastic pot in the top of the cylinder is an aid to watering: water is poured into the pot and then trickles down through the moss*

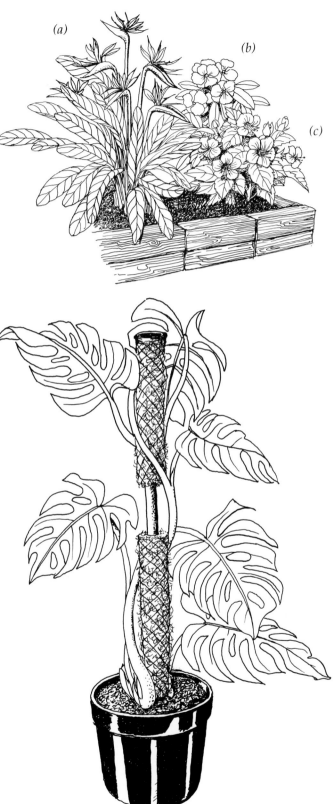

LEFT
Another aspect of the 'sheltered garden' is growing under cover, for example, in greenhouses and conservatories. Conservatories were very popular in the Victorian period (this is a superb example of a Victorian design). They then suffered a period of neglect, but are now more popular than ever before (BLAGDON HOUSE, SURREY)

RIGHT
Today there is a wide range of conservatories to choose from, including, at the top end of the market, modular structures in traditional styles. A typical example is shown here. These can be tailored by the manufacturer to suit the customers' requirements (WOODHILL, SURREY)

BELOW
Raised beds are attractive, and can be constructed after the conservatory base. They can be built up with various materials, such as bricks or ornamental concrete walling blocks. This bed is in a cool conservatory and contains stocks (ROYAL HORTICULTURAL SOCIETY'S GARDEN, SURREY)

Staging

Tiered staging can be used for displaying pot plants in a garden room. It can either be positioned against the back wall, or two units can be placed back to back in the centre of the building, space permitting.

Supporting climbers

Climbing plants will need some means of support. A system of horizontal galvanised or plastic-coated wires fixed to the back wall of the conservatory and up into the roof area is a good idea. Support the

wires with metal vine eyes, which will hold them at approximately 5cm (2in) away from the wall. This allows good air circulation behind the plants.

Alternatively, trellis panels could be fixed to the back wall, again ensuring there is a gap of 5cm (2in). Ornamental trellis panels are available in many shapes and sizes in timber, plastic or plastic-coated steel.

A moss pole makes an attractive support for climbers which produce aerial roots from their stems, like philodendrons, scindapsus and monstera. This can be positioned in a soil bed or in a tub and is easily made. It consists of a broom handle or wooden pole inserted firmly in the bed or tub. Then a cylinder of small-mesh wire netting is placed over it. The cylinder is filled with sphagnum moss, which is kept constantly moist, so encouraging the plant's stems to root into it. A good way of supplying moisture is to insert a plastic plant pot in the top of the cylinder so that its rim is level with the top of the wire netting. Water is simply poured into the pot, when it will trickle down through the moss.

A plant tree is a novel but very practical way of displaying epiphytic or tree-dwelling plants, like many of the bromeliads (shown here). It simply consists of a well-branched tree branch, which can be cemented into a pot

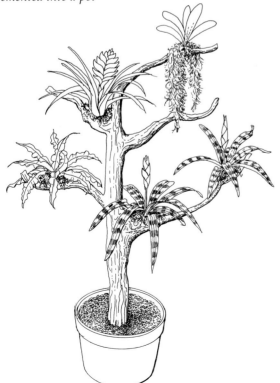

A plant tree

A plant tree is a marvellous way of displaying epiphytic or tree-dwelling plants, such as many of the bromeliads (see p.140). It consists of a well-branched tree branch, of whatever height you require. This can be inserted upright in a soil bed, or can be cemented into a large clay pot or tub.

The plants are then positioned in the crotches of the 'tree' and on the branches. Generally they have to be held in place with thin copper or plastic-coated wire, or nylon string, but make sure you do not tie them tightly, and use the tying materials as inconspicuously as possible.

Some bromeliads are supplied in pots, so before mounting them on the tree remove them from their containers, wash away all the soil and then surround the roots with moist live sphagnum moss. The air plants or atmospheric tillandsias must on no account have moss placed around the roots (if, indeed, they have any).

Eventually the plants will secure themselves to the tree with their roots. To water the plants, regularly spray them and the tree itself with water.

Hanging containers

Hanging baskets and other containers are well worth considering for displaying pendulous plants, such as the Sword Fern, *Nephrolepis exaltata;* trailing fuchsias, scindapsus and impatiens (which have a cascading habit when grown in baskets). Traditional wire hanging baskets lined with moss are not suitable for garden rooms as they drip water; instead use the modern moulded-plastic type complete with drip tray.

THE COOL CONSERVATORY

Most people will want to heat their conservatories so that they can grow a wider range of plants. Heating, of course, is expensive, so if you want to keep the costs down consider maintaining a cool conservatory – that is, with a minimum winter temperature of 4.5-7°C (40-45°F). This will enable you to grow a good range of the hardier (although frost-tender) plants.

A cool conservatory has to be very carefully managed in the winter as the atmosphere must be kept as dry as possible when temperatures are low. A little ventilation will help on all favourable occasions. Do not splash water about nor provide the plants with humidity.

Flowering shrubs

There is a number of excellent flowering shrubs for the cool conservatory, including camellias which bloom in winter or spring according to variety. Choose varieties of *C. japonica*, *C.* x *williamsii* and *C. reticulata*. Grow in tubs of acid compost and keep the plants outdoors after flowering, until the autumn, in a sheltered spot with partial shade.

The bottle-brush-like flowers of the evergreen Australian callistemon (Bottle Brush) give a flamboyant touch in the summer. The flowers of species like *C. citrinus*, *C. linearis*, *C. rigidus*, *C. speciosus* and *C. subulatus* are red. The plants are easily grown in beds or tubs of acid (lime-free) compost, airy conditions and sun. Stand tub-plants outdoors for the summer when flowering is over to help ripen new growth.

The evergreen coprosmas from New Zealand are little-known at present, but quite a few are now available and make excellent cool-conservatory specimens. Provide light shade in summer and good ventilation. Recommended species include *C. lucida* with shiny foliage and orange-red berries; and *C. robusta* 'Williamsii' with cream-edged leaves and similar berries. There are many hybrids like golden-variegated 'Beatson's Gold' and brown-leaved 'Chocolate Soldier'. Grow male and female plants together if you require plants to produce berries.

Although flamboyant in appearance, *Erythrina crista-galli* (Coral Tree) is easy to grow. The tall spiny stems carry deep red pea-shaped flowers in summer. The plant rests over winter, when it should be kept dry; in the spring cut down the dead stems almost to soil level.

Flowering climbers

Another plant with red pea-like flowers, but this time a climber, is *Clianthus puniceus* (Parrot's Bill). It grows only about 1.8m (6ft) in height. It needs very bright light but shade from strongest sun, and very well-drained soil.

One of the most popular conservatory climbers is *Hoya carnosa* (Wax Flower), an evergreen with pendulous clusters of white waxy blooms in summer. Growth is rather slow, so it is ideal for a small conservatory. If possible grow it in a soil bed or border in peat-rich soil. If you grow it in pots, use peat-based potting compost. It needs high humidity and light shade in summer.

Another highly popular climber (so much so that it is inclined to be in short supply at times) is *Lapageria rosea* (Chilean Bellflower) with large pendulous bell-shaped, waxy crimson flowers in late summer and autumn. This evergreen climber is best grown in a soil bed or border, but can be grown in a tub; the soil or compost must be lime-free and rich in peat. Provide light shade in summer.

For fragrance in the cool garden room a Jasmine is essential. Most usually grown is the white summer-flowering *Jasminum polyanthum*. Provide light shade in summer; prune out some of the older stems in late winter.

Flowering pot plants

These can be in flower all the year round. For instance, in winter and spring there are primulas, such as *P. malacoides*, *P. obconica* and *P.* x *kewensis*, all easily raised from seeds sown in the spring. Also flowering in winter and spring is *Senecio* x *hybridus* (Cineraria) with attractive daisy-like flowers, raised from seeds sown in spring. A stunning variety is 'Sky Blue' with flowers of that colour.

Schizanthus (Poor Man's Orchid) can be had in flower at almost any time and is easily raised from seed. It is valued for its profusion of orchid-like flowers. Pot-grown Lilies bloom in the spring or summer and can include such species as *Lilium auratum* with white and yellow flowers, the pink and white *L. regale*, pink and red *L. speciosum rubrum* and the white Easter Lily, *L. longiflorum*. Pot bulbs in the autumn. After flowering they can be planted in the garden.

Chrysanthemums herald the autumn and for display in the conservatory there are none finer than the Charm Chrysanthemums which are short bushy plants smothered with tiny daisy-like flowers. Cascade Chrysanthemums have a trailing habit and are ideal for displaying on tiered staging. The stems need guiding downwards with canes. Both can be raised from seeds or cuttings in early spring and are grown on outdoors till flowering time.

Foliage plants

Plants grown primarily for their foliage can be combined with flowering plants to act as a foil. A plant with very ferny green leaves is *Grevillea robusta* (Silk Oak), best grown in a pot, to keep it small, in lime-free soil-based potting compost. Hederas can be grown as climbers or trailers, allowing them to cascade over the edge of the staging. Varieties of the small-leaved *H. helix* are popular, both variegated or plain green. Of the large-leaved ivies, *H. canariensis* 'Gloire de Marengo' with variegated foliage is recommended. Best for shady conditions are the green-leaved kinds; variegated ivies need more light for best colour.

THE INTERMEDIATE CONSERVATORY

With a slightly higher minimum winter temperature of 10°C (50°F) a different range of plants can be grown. Conditions will be more comfortable for you, too, although 10°C is still a bit on the chilly side. Again you must keep the atmosphere dry in winter when conditions are cool, but humidity can be increased when the weather becomes warmer.

Flowering shrubs

Some exotic-looking yet easy shrubs for the intermediate conservatory include *Tibouchina semidecandra* (Glory Bush) with handsome velvety evergreen foliage, and sumptuous bluish-purple bowl-shaped flowers in summer and autumn. It is versatile, growing equally well in a soil bed or pot, amenable to hard pruning to keep it small, and suitable for training on the back wall if a large specimen is required. Shade it lightly in summer.

Equally spectacular is *Brunfelsia calycina*, an evergreen with large blue-purple flowers in summer. Grow in a tub or soil bed and provide light shade in summer. Most conservatory owners want to grow an oleander, *Nerium oleander*. This evergreen shrub with pink, red or purplish blooms in summer and autumn is easy enough; its basic needs are airy conditions and plenty of sun. The plant can go outside for the summer if pot grown.

The deciduous shrub *Hibiscus rosa-sinensis* is truly spectacular in summer when it produces a succession of large trumpet-shaped flowers. Usually varieties are grown, in shades of red, pink, orange, yellow and white. Shade it lightly in summer, provide high humidity and in late winter prune it back if you wish to keep the plant small.

There are a few shrubs which are only suitable for large conservatories, including datura (Angel's Trumpets) with huge trumpet-shaped flowers in summer and autumn. They are cream in the species *D. cornigera* and its double variety *D.c.* 'Knightii', and bright orange-red in *D. sanguinea*. Shade lightly in summer and in late winter cut down the previous

year's stems to within 15cm (6in) of the soil.

Another very large shrub is the evergreen *Sparmannia africana* (African Hemp) with big heart-shaped leaves and white flowers in spring and summer. Growing it in a tub will restrict its size. Shade it lightly in summer.

Although quite tall the cestrums can be grown in the small garden room by training them up the back wall. Evergreen or semi-evergreen species recommended are orange *C. aurantiacum*, red *C. elegans* and *C.* 'Newellii', and pink *C. roseum*. All have bunches of tubular flowers in summer. Provide light shade in summer; and in late winter prune out all stems which are three years old.

Abutilons can also be trained flat on the back wall. They flower in summer, producing pendulous bell-like blooms. Normally hybrids are grown, like the red 'Ashford Red', yellow 'Canary Bird' and 'Golden Fleece', and orange-red 'Firebell'. Cut the stems back fairly hard in early spring.

The small evergreen shrub *Lantana camara* has an incredibly long flowering period: it produces its rounded heads of yellow flowers throughout summer and autumn. The flowers turn to pink or red as they age. There are varieties with flowers in other colours: shades of red, pink, or yellow. It needs a lot of sun, and can be pruned back hard in early spring.

Flowering climbers

Top of the popularity charts is bougainvillea (Paper Flower) which produces highly colourful paper-like bracts (modified leaves) in the summer. With purple-red bracts is *B. glabra*, while *B. spectabilis* comes in red or purple. There are hybrids available, too, like 'Mrs Butt' (crimson); 'Orange Glow'; 'Red Emperor'; and 'Dania' (double red). It needs plenty of sunshine. Prune it back by one-third in early spring if you want to reduce its height.

Plumbago capensis is also high in the popularity charts and suitable for small garden rooms. It produces pale blue flowers in summer and autumn. Provide light shade in summer; in late winter cut

In a conservatory or garden room staging can be used to display pot plants. This is single-level staging, but tiered staging allows even more ambitious displays. This intermediate conservatory contains a wide range of plants, including cacti, succulents and pelargoniums (INVEREWE GARDEN, SCOTLAND, NATIONAL TRUST FOR SCOTLAND)

back lateral shoots and reduce the height of main stems.

Every conservatory owner, it seems, wants to grow a Passion Flower, but bear in mind that growth is very vigorous. The usual one grown is the Blue Passion Flower, *Passiflora caerulea*. Provide light shade in summer. In late winter thin out the oldest stems and reduce lateral shoots to 15cm (6in).

Best grown in a soil bed or border is *Mandevilla laxa (M. suaveolens)* (Chilean Jasmine) with funnel-shaped, white, highly scented flowers in summer. Provide light shade in summer.

The Climbing Lily, *Gloriosa rothschildiana*, has red and yellow lily-like blooms in summer. It is a tuberous plant, and tubers should be potted in spring. Shade it lightly in summer. In autumn dry off the tubers and store them in the conservatory.

Flowering pot plants

These can be used to give colour throughout the year. Top of the list for autumn and winter colour are the varieties of *Cyclamen persicum* with flowers in shades of red, pink, white, etc. Many varieties have very attractive silver-marbled foliage. They grow from tubers and can be kept for many years. Dry them off for the summer.

For spring colour try *Clivia miniata,* a perennial with heads of tubular orange flowers. It flowers better when pot-bound. Hydrangeas bloom in spring under glass. Use the mop-headed varieties of *H. macrophylla* with blue or pink flowers. It is best to raise new plants each year from cuttings taken in spring. They are good for shade.

For summer, fuchsias are highly popular: bush forms for pots, trailing kinds for baskets. Like hydrangeas, they are best raised each year from cuttings taken in spring. Shade them lightly from strong sun.

Easily raised from seeds sown in spring are various summer-flowering pot plants which are discarded after flowering, like browallia with blue or white tubular flowers; varieties of *Celosia plumosa* (Prince of Wales' Feathers) with red or yellow plumes; and impatiens (Busy Lizzie) with single or double blooms in shades of red, orange, pink and white, which is ideal for shade.

The regal pelargoniums, varieties of *P. domesticum*, are popular and freely produce flowers in shades of pink, red, mauve, purple and white. Raise new plants each year from cuttings in late summer. They need plenty of sun.

Streptocarpus (Cape Primrose) can be grown as a perennial, producing tubular blooms in various colours during summer. Plants should be kept dryish over winter while resting.

A flamboyant yet easily grown perennial, *Strelitzia reginae* (Bird of Paradise Flower) has large dramatic foliage and orange and blue flowers in summer, which are shaped like a bird's head. Flowering will not commence until plants are at least five years old. They need plenty of sun. Eventually they will need a tub; or plant them in a soil bed.

Zantedeschia aethiopica (Arum Lily) is a perennial, growing from fleshy rhizomes, with bold arrow-shaped leaves and white sail-like flowers in the summer. Other species include *Z. elliottiana* with yellow flowers. Also worth looking out for is a new group of *Z. aethiopica* varieties from New Zealand with flowers in shades of pink, yellow, red and orange. Keep *Z. aethiopica* and varieties moist all year round, but dry off others for the winter.

The bromeliads (relations of the pineapple) are extremely diverse in habit and are becoming as popular as cacti. The epiphytic (tree-dwelling) atmospheric tillandsias (air plants) should be grown on a plant tree (see p.136). Other epiphytes can be grown either in pots or on a tree. They include the brown-banded *Vriesia splendens* (Flaming Sword); the red-centred *Nidularium fulgens;* and *Aechmea fasciata* (Urn Plant), with grey foliage. Epiphytic bromeliads generally produce spectacular spikes of highly coloured flowers and bracts.

Terrestrial bromeliads, which are always grown in pots, include the cryptanthus (Earth Stars) which have rosettes of attractively marked leaves. *Ananas comosus* 'Variegatus', the Variegated Pineapple, has a rosette of cream-edged leaves which are very spiny.

Bromeliads grown on a plant tree are watered by spraying them and the tree with water (ideally rainwater). Spray daily in warm conditions, weekly when temperatures are low. Some bromeliads form their leaves into water-holding vases, including vriesia, nidularium and aechmea. These 'vases' should be kept filled with fresh rainwater. Bromeliads like high humidity in warm conditions and good light but shade from strong sun. When grown in pots use a peat-based compost and do not pot on until plants become pot-bound. They only require small pots.

Foliage plants

One of the most useful foliage plants for the intermediate conservatory, to use as a foil for flowering plants, is *Asparagus densiflorus* 'Sprengeri', a pendulous plant with bright green needle-like branchlets. Use it liberally among any flowering pot plants and especially to 'soften' the edges of the staging.

Hederas have already been described (see The cool conservatory, p.136) but are suitable too for slightly warmer conditions. *Sansevieria trifasciata* 'Laurentii' must be included for its dramatic, yellow-edged sword-like leaves. It is commonly known as Mother-in-law's Tongue, and is one of the few plants which tolerates a dry atmosphere. Water sparingly and ensure it is in really bright light.

THE WARM CONSERVATORY

In the warm conservatory a temperature range of 15.5-21°C (60-70°F) is maintained all the year round. Most people would agree that this provides the most comfortable conditions for living in; and it is ideal, too, for a vast range of tropical and sub-tropical plants. The majority of these need high humidity, though, and although they like good light they should be shaded from the strongest sun.

Flowering shrubs

There are several spectacular plants in this category, including *Aphelandra squarrosa* 'Louisae' (Zebra Plant) with white-striped foliage and heads of long-lasting yellow bracts; *Crossandra infundibuliformis* with brilliant orange-red blooms in summer; and *Gardenia jasminoides* (Cape Jasmine), with highly fragrant white blooms in summer and autumn. All are evergreen.

Flowering climbers

Warmth-loving climbers are equally impressive, such as *Allamanda cathartica* with huge brilliant yellow trumpet-shaped blooms in summer and autumn; *Dipladenia splendens (Mandevilla splendens)* (Pink Allamanda), with deep pink trumpet-shaped blooms in summer; and *Stephanotis floribunda* (Madagascar Jasmine), with white waxy highly fragrant flowers for most of the year (except winter). With these climbers previous year's growth should be cut back to within a few buds in early spring. All are evergreen.

Flowering pot plants

Perennial flowering pot plants which can be kept for many years, and which add an exotic touch to the warm garden room, include the anthuriums with highly colourful spathes (bracts). *A. andreanum* has scarlet or red spathes, although there are now varieties in other colours. *A. scherzerianum* has brilliant scarlet spathes.

The ever-popular saintpaulias (African Violets) are suitable for the warm conservatory provided high humidity can be maintained around them. Grow them in small pots of peat-based compost. As well as the usual varieties with single or double flowers in many colours, micro-miniatures (very tiny plants) and trailing kinds are also available.

Foliage plants

There is a vast range of suitable foliage plants, both perennials and shrubs, and indeed they should feature strongly in the warm conservatory. There are so many that all one can do is briefly describe them. The following are recommended.

Aglaonema commutatum varieties (Chinese Evergreens), foliage boldly marked silver or white; *Begonia rex*, multicoloured foliage; *Calathea zebrina*, emerald-green velvety foliage; *Codiaeum variegatum pictum*, multicoloured foliage; *Cordyline terminalis*, red or purplish sword-shaped leaves; *Dieffenbachia maculata* and *D. exotica* (Dumb Cane), cream or white splashed leaves; *Ficus lyrata* (Fiddleback Fig), with large spoon-shaped leaves; *Ficus benjamina* (Weeping Fig), pendulous branches; *Monstera deliciosa* (Swiss Cheese Plant), large perforated and deeply cut foliage, a climber; peperomias (Pepper Elders), small clump-forming plants, variable foliage; philodendrons, mainly climbers with large leaves, often deeply cut or lobed, or heart-shaped; and *Scindapsus aureus* (Devil's Ivy), a climber with yellow-marbled leaves.

Ferns are recommended, too, and undoubtedly one of the most popular is the Sword Fern, *Nephrolepis exaltata*, with arching light green fronds. Every garden room should have a palm. Of the various species available one could not do much better than grow *Howea belmoreana* or *H. forsterana* with dark green feathery foliage. They are tall-growing kinds.

TIPS ON PLANT CARE

Conservatory plants, with very few exceptions, must be shaded from the strongest sun to prevent leaf and

flower scorch. This is best achieved by fitting the conservatory with a set of external roller blinds.

Good ventilation, consistent with maintaining the minimum temperatures, is necessary all the year round. In spring and summer one often needs to ventilate freely to keep temperatures down. When buying a conservatory make sure it is fitted with plenty of roof ventilators and side ventilators. Open both for a good through-flow of air.

The majority of conservatory plants need humidity or moist air around them when conditions are warm. In a conservatory which is used as a living area it is impractical to make the entire atmosphere humid, as this is uncomfortable. Instead provide 'local humidity' immediately around the plants.

Plants in pots can be stood in shallow plastic trays containing a horticultural aggregate or gravel, which should be kept constantly moist. This will result in humid air rising around the plants. Do not, however, allow pots to stand in water.

Plants in beds, tubs and hanging containers, and climbers on the back wall, can be mist-sprayed daily or twice daily in warm weather, using a hand sprayer. Try to use rainwater for this if your tapwater is hard.

The Productive Garden

Most books on fruit and vegetable growing will tell you that the majority of these crops give best results when grown in a warm sheltered site. This is borne out by gardeners of old who often grew fruits and vegetables in walled gardens, especially in large gardens and estates. Some people are lucky enough to possess an old walled garden, which should certainly be used for culinary crops if possible. Otherwise any warm well-sheltered area of the garden will do, provided it is open to the sky and receives plenty of sun.

Growth of fruits and vegetables is very much better if they are sheltered from the wind, as plants are not liable to be damaged or loosened in the soil. In calm conditions the soil dries out less quickly so the plants are less likely to suffer from moisture deficit.

Warm sheltered conditions allow for early sowings of vegetables and result in early maturity. However, early fruit blossoms may need protecting from late-spring frosts. These can kill fruit blossoms and, of course, this results in little or no fruit being produced.

GROWING UNDER COVER

Even more protection in cool climates can be provided in the form of glass and polythene – greenhouses, frames and cloches. Such protection allows for even earlier sowings of vegetables and ensures tender kinds make faster growth and start cropping earlier. Many vegetables can be started off in a greenhouse and later planted out in the garden. Others can be sown in situ and covered with cloches to give them a head start in life. Tender vegetables like tomatoes, sweet peppers and aubergines will do very much better if grown throughout their entire lives under glass or polythene, especially in cool climates.

Greenhouses for vegetables

A very useful and economically priced 'greenhouse' for vegetable growing is the polythene tunnel. The framework consists of galvanised tubular-steel hoops inserted in the ground; these are covered with a flexible polythene 'skin'. Tunnels are not generally heated as they quickly lose heat. They usually have a door at each end for ventilation and access, and a central path could be created from one to the other (simply a beaten-earth path, or paving slabs loosely laid). This will create a long border on each side of the tunnel in which vegetables can be grown.

If you want to heat the greenhouse then opt for a glass structure as this is better at retaining heat. For vegetables a structure with glass to ground level is best as it lets in more light. Choose either a traditional span-roof greenhouse, or a Dutch-light design which has large panes of glass and sloping sides, resulting in very high light intensity within.

In a walled garden erect a lean-to greenhouse on the sunniest wall as this retains heat even better than a free-standing greenhouse (the wall actually stores heat during the day and slowly releases it again at night). Because of this a lean-to is economical to heat artificially. Again, choose a model with glass to ground level.

Try to site a tunnel or free-standing greenhouse so that the ridge runs from east to west. Make sure that it is not overshadowed by trees or large buildings; choose an open situation which receives plenty of sunshine for as much of the day as possible.

Cloches

These low structures, used to cover plants, are especially useful for vegetable growing and for strawberries. They not only provide weather protection, but also help to extend the vegetable season, providing early and late crops.

Various types of cloches are available. The tent cloche generally consists of two panes of glass (or rigid plastic) held together in tent formation with wire clips or fittings. The cloches are placed end to end to form a continuous row and the ends are closed with sheets of glass or plastic. They are low structures, suitable only for low-growing crops like lettuces, carrots, radishes and strawberries.

Barn cloches are taller, consisting of four sheets of glass (or rigid plastic) held together with special wire clips or fittings. They are placed end to end to form a continuous row. They resemble a traditional-style greenhouse in shape, and are ideal for taller crops like bush tomatoes, sweet corn, peas, etc.

Low polythene tunnels consist of long sheets of clear or white polythene stretched over galvanised-wire hoops and held in place with thinner wire hoops or string. The ends of the polythene are buried in the soil or tied to wooden pegs.

A comparatively new idea is the floating cloche, simply polythene film with thousands of tiny slits in it. It is placed over a seed bed after sowing vegetables, or it can be laid over newly planted vegetables. It is laid very loosely and the edges are buried in the soil. As the plants grow they lift the polythene and the slits gradually open. Floating cloches can be kept over plants right up to harvesting time if desired – at least, in the case of low-growing vegetables.

As with greenhouses, cloches should be sited in a sunny spot.

Cloches are invaluable in the vegetable garden. They can cover newly sown seeds or newly planted young plants and be left in place until the plants are well established. Then they can be transferred to other crops which would benefit from protection (see the table, p.148). A system known as strip cropping is particularly useful. This minimises movement of cloches. For instance, you could mark out

The polythene tunnel is often used for growing vegetables in cool temperate climates. It is a very simple and economically priced structure, consisting of tubular-steel hoops inserted in the ground and covered with a flexible polythene 'skin'

three parallel strips of ground for each row of cloches, with paths between. The row of cloches is moved from one strip to another as required for covering crops. To give an example: sow seeds in the first strip and cover with cloches; when the plants are established and growing well, sow seeds in the second strip and move the cloches over these; when these plants are established sow the third strip and move the cloches across.

Garden frames
These, like cloches, are low structures for covering and protecting plants, but they provide more headroom than cloches.

There are several types available, including the single-span frame which, like a lean-to greenhouse, is designed to be placed against a sunny wall. A double-span frame is more like a traditional span-roof greenhouse in shape, although much lower. There are many proprietary models of both types, with timber or aluminium frames and clad in glass or plastic. As with greenhouses, it is best to opt for those which have glass to ground level, rather than those with solid sides, as they let in more light.

Garden frames are used for hardening plants which have been raised in heated greenhouses, prior to planting outside (for example, tomatoes, marrows, sweet corn, cucumbers, melons, aubergines and sweet peppers).

Garden frames can also be used for growing crops to maturity, resulting in earlier harvesting, as can be seen in the table on p.148.

VEGETABLES WHICH NEED SHELTERED CONDITIONS
Some vegetables can be grown in quite open, exposed conditions and still perform and crop well. However, there are others which are best grown in sheltered conditions, perhaps to ensure they are not blown over or loosened in the soil, or because they are tender or delicate and therefore need a warm, wind-free spot in order to do well. The following vegetables should certainly be pampered!

Brussels sprouts
As these are tall plants they need shelter from strong winds otherwise they are liable to be blown over or severely loosened in the soil. In the latter instance,

YEAR-ROUND CROPPING PROGRAMME FOR VEGETABLES UNDER CLOCHES

Crop	Sow/plant cloches on	Cloches removed	Harvesting time
Beans, French and Runner	Sow and cover late spring	Early summer	Mid- to late summer onwards
Beans, Broad	Sow and cover late autumn	Mid-spring	Late spring
Beetroots	Sow and cover mid-spring	Late spring or early summer	Summer
Brussels Sprouts	Sow and cover early spring	Mid-spring	Autumn onwards
Cabbage, summer	Sow and cover early spring	Mid-spring	Summer
Carrots, early varieties	Sow and cover early spring	Mid-spring	Early summer
Cauliflower, summer	Sow and cover early autumn	Mid-spring	Early summer
Cucumber, outdoor	Plant and cover late spring	End of cropping period	Summer to early autumn
Leeks	Sow and cover early spring	Mid-spring	Autumn and winter
Lettuce, summer	Sow and cover early to mid-spring	Late spring or early summer	Early summer onwards
Marrows	Plant and cover late spring	Early summer	Summer and autumn
Onion, salad	Sow and cover early autumn	Mid-spring	Spring
Peas, early varieties	Sow and cover mid-autumn	Mid-spring	Spring to early summer
Radishes	Sow and cover early spring	Mid-spring	Mid-spring
Spinach, summer	Sow and cover early spring	Mid- to late spring	Late spring and summer
Sweet Corn	Plant and cover late spring	Early summer	Summer
Tomatoes, dwarf bush	Plant and cover late spring	When plants outgrow cloches	Late summer to mid-autumn

VEGETABLES TO GROW TO MATURITY IN GARDEN FRAMES

Crop	Plant or sow	Harvest
Aubergine	Plant late spring	Summer and into autumn
Bean, Dwarf French	Sow mid- to late spring	Early to mid-summer
Beetroots	Sow early spring	Early summer
Capsicum (Sweet Pepper)	Plant late spring	Summer to early autumn
Carrots, early varieties	Sow late winter or early spring	Late spring onwards
Chicory, sugar-loaf type	Sow during summer	Autumn and winter
Corn salad	Sow early autumn	Autumn
Cucumber, frame types	Plant late spring	Summer
Endive	Sow late summer	Autumn and early winter
Lettuce, overwintering varieties	Sow late summer to early autumn	Autumn, winter, spring, according to variety
Onion, Spring	Sow late summer	Winter and spring
Parsley	Sow late summer or early spring	Autumn or spring
Radish	Sow late winter or early spring	Early spring onwards
Spinach, winter	Sow late summer or early autumn	Winter
Tomato, bush varieties	Plant late spring	Summer to early autumn
Turnip, early varieties	Sow late winter to early spring	Late spring onwards

the sprouts will not then develop properly and will be loose and open, unfit for the table.

For best results grow in full sun (although slight shade is tolerated) and in firm soil to ensure the roots are well anchored. Really firm planting is recommended. Sow them in mid-spring; harvest in autumn and winter.

Winter cauliflowers
Some varieties are not too hardy and succumb to a severe winter, so are best grown only in mild areas and certainly in very sheltered conditions. In this instance it is possible to have cauliflowers on the Christmas dinner table.

Avoid very wet soils, too, as these conditions can also lead to death in the winter. Although a fertile soil is recommended, do not overfeed with nitrogen which results in soft growth unable to withstand cold winter weather. Several leaves should be bent over the developing heads, again to protect from winter weather. Sow them in mid-spring; harvest in winter or spring.

Sprouting broccoli
This is a good alternative to winter cauliflowers as it is much hardier, but nevertheless needs a position sheltered from winds as, due to its tall habit of growth, it is easily blown over or loosened in the soil. There are purple and white varieties. It is an ideal choice, too, if the soil is on the poor side. Sow it in mid-spring; harvest in winter and spring.

Calabrese
Also known as green sprouting broccoli, and similar in habit to sprouting broccoli, this popular brassica forms a large, green, cauliflower-like flower head. It is not as hardy as sprouting broccoli and needs a warm sheltered position to do well. From a sowing in mid-spring the heads will be ready for harvesting between late summer and mid-autumn. Secondary flower heads are produced after the main head has been cut. These can continue until severe frosts occur.

Kale
Although the kales, whether curly or plain-leaved, are very hardy, growth is much better if the plants are grown in a sheltered spot. The plants are tall, so are liable to be blown over or loosened in the soil in an exposed windy garden. They are suitable for poor or fertile soils. Seeds are sown in mid-spring; plants should be well firmed in when transplanting; and harvesting takes place from autumn to spring.

French beans
French beans, whether climbing or dwarf varieties, must be grown in warm sheltered conditions as they are half-hardy annuals. If desired, dwarf kinds can be grown to maturity in garden frames, while these or climbing kinds will relish the conditions provided by a polythene tunnel or greenhouse. In cool climates under cover they will grow quicker and crop much earlier than outdoor plants. Grow them in fertile moisture-retentive soil. Sow in mid- to late spring and harvest in summer. For successful germination a soil temperature of at least 10°C (50°F) is required.

Runner beans
Runner beans are grown as half-hardy annuals and are prone to frost damage in spring and autumn. Sowings should not be made outside until late spring if there is risk of frost, but plants can be raised under glass in mid-spring and planted out when danger of frost is over. Harvesting takes place in summer and through to autumn. A moisture-retentive fertile soil gives best results. A warm, sheltered, sunny site is essential because runner beans are climbers and easily damaged by wind. Furthermore, a sheltered sunny site is favoured by insects which pollinate the flowers; this is essential for crops to be produced.

Broad beans
These hardy annuals need a sheltered site to prevent them being blown over or battered by winds, due to their height. They can be grown in exposed positions, but in this instance need some means of support. There are winter-hardy varieties available which can be sown in late autumn to provide pickings in late spring or early summer. However, the main sowings are made in early to mid-spring for summer crops. Grow them in fertile well-drained soil; overwintering beans will not survive wet or waterlogged soils. The minimum soil temperature for germination of seeds is 5°C (39°F).

Peas
These hardy annuals come in both tall and dwarf varieties, the former, especially, needing a sheltered

site to prevent them being blown over. The hardiest peas are the round-seeded varieties which can be sown outside in late autumn to provide pickings in early summer. The less-hardy wrinkle-seeded varieties are sown in spring for summer crops. Provide a fertile, well-drained, yet moisture-retentive soil. Soils which lie wet over winter are anathema to overwintering peas.

Marrows

Marrows, including courgettes, are frost-tender plants needing a warm, sunny, sheltered site to crop well. Soil drainage must be good. Plants can be raised under glass in mid-spring and planted out when danger of frost is over. Alternatively outdoor sowings can be made in late spring. Cropping takes place in summer and into autumn, and will be curtailed by the first frosts of autumn.

Sweet Corn

This half-hardy annual is grown for its corn cobs. Best results are obtained in high temperatures with plenty of sunshine. A warm sheltered site is essential. Numerous varieties which crop well in cool temperate climates are now available. Grow them in a well-drained, fertile, yet moisture-retentive soil. In cool temperate climates sowings are generally made under glass in mid-spring and the young plants set out when danger of frost is over. Outdoor sowings should take place in late spring, once the soil temperature has reached 10-13°C (50-55°F). Plants should be grown in blocks rather than rows as this ensures better pollination of the flowers. The cobs should be ready for harvesting from late summer onwards.

Potatoes

Although suitable for cool temperate climates, the potato originates from South America and is half-hardy and easily damaged by frost. Late spring frosts will kill newly emerged shoots and foliage and mature top growth in autumn. In cool temperate climates potatoes are planted in spring: early varieties in early spring; second-early and main-crop varieties a few weeks later. Potatoes should on no account be planted in frost-pockets (low spots into which cold air drains). They relish deep, fertile, humus-rich soil with good drainage.

Tomatoes

These frost-tender plants can be grown in cool temperate climates. In this instance they are generally grown in a heated or cold greenhouse, mainly for summer fruit production. There are, however, outdoor varieties for cool temperate climates which can be grown without any protection, again for summer cropping.

The usual programme consists of sowing seeds in a heated greenhouse in early to mid-spring in a temperature of 18-21°C (65-70°F). Plants for outdoor cropping must not be set outside until all danger of frost is over (usually late spring or early summer). For these, a really warm, sunny, sheltered spot is recommended for best results. Most success is achieved with outdoor plants in milder areas with warm summers. Dwarf bush varieties can be grown in garden frames. A fertile, well-drained, yet moisture-retentive soil gives best results.

Sweet peppers and aubergines

Like tomatoes, these are also frost-tender plants and are grown in the same way. In cool temperate climates best results are achieved under glass or polythene. As they are not particularly tall plants they can be recommended for large garden frames.

FRUITS WHICH NEED SHELTERED CONDITIONS

As with some vegetables, certain fruits, although hardy, perform better in warm sheltered conditions. The site needs to be wind-free to encourage pollinating insects to do their job of transferring pollen from flower to flower, to ensure bumper crops of fruits. Avoid growing fruits in frost-pockets (low-lying areas into which cold air drains) as frost can damage early flowers which results in few or no fruits being produced. Plenty of sun is required for good growth and ripening of fruits, although soft fruits will still perform well in partial shade – for instance, a site which receives sun for half a day. For details of wall-trained fruits, see Chapter 6, p.93.

Strawberries

These are among the most popular of the soft fruits; the plants are hardy (Z6) although spring frosts can kill the flowers. In areas prone to spring frosts it pays to grow strawberries under cloches. The cloches can be put over the plants in mid-winter and removed in early summer. Planted in late summer, the plants will then crop in late spring and early summer the following year.

The strawberry is a versatile fruit and is grown in various climates, from the tropics to cool temperate regions. There are both summer- and autumn-fruiting varieties.

The best results are obtained in well-drained yet moisture-retentive fertile soil. The ideal planting time is mid- to late summer for good crops the following year. Varieties fruiting in the autumn are best covered with cloches during that season in temperate climates. Plant them 45cm (18in) apart in rows.

These days, however, with small gardens being commonplace, many people grow strawberries intensively in containers to save space. The traditional method of planting them in rows 75-90cm (2½-3ft) apart in the vegetable or fruit plot is extremely space consuming.

Strawberries in containers can make good patio features, especially if grown in decorative tubs or pots, as they are not unattractive plants. They are ideal for balcony and roof gardens, too, if lightweight containers are chosen.

Proprietary lightweight plastic strawberry containers are available. They are tallish tower-like units – cylinders with planting pockets in the sides.

Another way of growing strawberries intensively is in a barrel. A heavy wooden barrel can be used and looks attractive in a more informal setting. If weight is a problem, consider using a plastic rainwater butt, which is shaped very much like a barrel.

The barrel or butt should have 5cm (2in) diameter holes drilled in the sides, in a staggered formation and spaced about 20cm (8in) apart each way. Do not forget to drill some holes in the base also to ensure surplus water is able to drain away. As you are filling the barrel with compost (ideally soil-based potting compost, but peat-based if weight is a problem) carefully push the roots of the strawberry plants through the holes in the sides and spread them out well before covering with compost. When the barrel or butt has been filled (leave a 5cm (2in) space at the top for watering) finish off by planting a few plants in the top.

With proprietary strawberry containers, follow the supplier's instructions for planting.

Make sure the compost does not dry out; keep it steadily moist as strawberries do not like to go short of water.

Raspberries

Raspberries (Z6-9) are also highly popular soft fruits and an ideal choice for a small garden as they take up minimum lateral space and crop heavily. Winds can damage the tall canes (stems) and deter pollinating insects, so this is why a well-sheltered site is recommended. They are excellent for partial shade.

There are both summer-fruiting and autumn-fruiting varieties, both of which grow well in fertile, moisture-retentive, well-drained soil. Plant them 30cm (12in) apart in rows. The tall canes should be supported with a system of posts and wires. Immediately summer-fruiting raspberries have finished cropping, the old fruited canes are cut down to ground level and the new canes tied in to their supports. Autumn-fruiting raspberries are pruned in late winter by cutting down all canes to ground level. The new canes produced in spring will then crop in autumn. Ideally try to provide a site which receives sun all day long for autumn-fruiting varieties as this results in more fruits ripening.

Blackcurrants

These hardy soft fruits are fairly popular, although they take up quite a bit of ground; the bushes need to be planted 1.5-1.8m (5-6ft) apart each way. They need a sheltered spot to ensure pollinating insects do their job, and try to ensure the site is frost-free because the early spring flowers can be damaged by late frosts. A position in partial shade is acceptable (Z6-9)

Blackcurrants need a fertile, well-drained yet moisture-retentive soil. In areas prone to late-spring frosts grow only late-flowering varieties. It would also help to cover plants with fine-mesh netting at night to protect the flowers from frost. Prune bushes in early autumn by cutting out old wood which has carried fruits, as near to the base of the plant as possible. Leave plenty of young shoots as these bear fruit the following year.

Gooseberries

As with blackcurrants, gooseberry bushes are hardy (Z6-9) but nevertheless should be grown in a sheltered site, free from wind, and avoiding frost-pockets. The flowers are produced in mid-spring so are liable to damage from late frosts unless protected. Partial shade is acceptable. Plant in fertile well-drained soil, setting the bushes 1.5m (5ft) apart each way. Pruning consists of cutting back all lateral shoots to five leaves in early to mid-summer. Then in winter reduce leading shoots by half their length. Laterals are further reduced to two buds of their base.

Melons

The melon is a tropical plant, a climbing annual, so in cool temperate regions is grown under glass. Cantaloup varieties are the most popular and can be grown in unheated greenhouses or frames. Seeds are sown under glass in mid-spring and germinated in a temperature of 18-21°C (65-70°F). Plant out in fertile soil when plants are approximately six weeks old. Generally one melon plant is set in the middle of each frame; in a greenhouse plants can be set 38cm (15in) apart in a row. In a frame, four side shoots are allowed to grow to each corner before the tips are pinched out: they trail over the ground. Greenhouse melons are trained vertically to a system of wires on one of the side walls. They can be allowed to grow to the ridge of the house. It is best to pollinate melon flowers by hand: simply dab the centres of female flowers with a male flower (the former have an embryo fruit behind them). In temperate climates fruits ripen in late summer and early autumn.

PRODUCTIVE CONTAINERS

One does not have to own a traditional garden in order to grow vegetables and fruits. Owners of balconies and roof gardens should be pleased to learn that many fruits and vegetables can be grown in containers, such as tubs, pots and growing-bags. Furthermore, garden owners who do not have sufficient ground for utility crops could consider container growing on the patio. There are, too, several ways of making vegetables and fruits in containers look more attractive, as features in their own right.

Vegetables

Containers for balconies and roof gardens should be light in weight, and here the growing-bag comes into its own. Ideal for many vegetables, growing-bags are long plastic bags (approximately 1.2m [4ft] in length) filled with lightweight, peat-based pot-

Growing-bags are an ideal arrangement for a balcony or roof garden. They can be hidden by surrounding them with small plants grown in pots. Use bushy or trailing summer bedding plants for this purpose, such as petunias

ting compost. They are not particularly attractive, but they can be hidden (see below). Growing-bags are strictly temporary, being used for only one crop or one growing season, after which they are discarded.

The bags are prepared for planting by cutting out circles or squares in the plastic top to make sufficiently large holes.

Growing-bags can be hidden by surrounding them with small plants grown in pots: ideal for this purpose are summer bedding plants of a bushy or trailing nature, such as petunias, lobelia, alyssum, verbena, ivy-leaved pelargoniums, mimulus and impatiens.

The growing-bags should be placed in a sunny position as most vegetables do not grow or crop too well in shade.

CHOOSING FOR COLOUR
Choosing colourful or otherwise attractive vegetables is sensible when growing on balconies, roof gardens and patios, as then they become pleasing features in their own right. For instance, beetroots have very attractive purple leaves and make a good

LEFT
In cool temperate climates grapes are probably best grown in a greenhouse. Generally, they are trained as single permanent stems up into the roof area. These stems produce fruit bearing laterals each year. After fruiting they are cut back to within a bud or two of their base (GARDEN IN HARTLEY WINTNEY, BERKSHIRE)

RIGHT
The sheltered border in front of this sunny wall makes an excellent site for fruits including dwarf apples and strawberries, while fan-trained fruits are grown on the wall itself (PEPER HAROW, SURREY)

foil for summer-flowering plants. For growing-bags it is best to choose varieties with small round roots rather than the long-rooted types. Sow them sparingly and thin the seedlings to 10cm (4in) apart each way.

Asparagus peas are extremely attractive, and very productive, too. They have a carpeting habit of growth and produce masses of red flowers, followed by winged pods. These are picked when approx. 5cm (2in) long and cooked whole. When sowing, space the seeds about 20cm (8in) apart each way.

French and runner beans are also suitable for growing-bags. Climbing French beans are far more productive than the dwarf varieties. The flowers are attractive, and so are the pods if purple-podded varieties are chosen. Set the seeds 10-15cm (4-6in) apart each way. The plants can be allowed to climb, say, up a wall-mounted trellis panel.

This is a good way to support runner beans, too. These are very attractive when in flower, producing masses of red, scarlet, pink or white flowers according to the variety grown. The seeds should be spaced 10-15cm (4-6in) apart each way.

Growing-bags are perfect for tomatoes. Many ornamental kinds are available, such as mini-fruited cherry-, currant-, plum- and pear-shaped varieties. They may have red or yellow fruits. There are larger-fruited yellow tomatoes, too, and even striped varieties. The normal-sized growing-bag will hold up to four tomato plants. Proprietary growing-bag crop supports are available which should be used for supporting tomatoes as one cannot insert bamboo canes into these containers.

Rhubarb chard, a leaf beet, is an unusual but very colourful and worthwhile vegetable for growing-bags. The stems are brilliant red and are cooked and eaten as a vegetable; the leaves are also used, like spinach. The normal-sized growing-bag will hold four or five plants.

Carrots should not be dismissed as being unattractive. Their ferny foliage makes a pleasing foil for brightly coloured summer-flowering bedding plants. Choose early stump- or round-rooted varieties, sow the seeds broadcast and thin seedlings to 5cm (2in) apart each way.

Colourful or attractive salad crops include non-hearting lettuces with deeply cut foliage, such as

'Salad Bowl'. The leaves are picked individually. It makes a good foil for summer bedding plants. There are also red-leaved lettuces. Four or five lettuces can be grown in the average growing-bag.

Chicory is another useful salad crop; the red variety 'Rossa de Verona' is very colourful. Grow four plants per bag.

Curled endive, with curly green foliage, is as attractive mixed with summer bedding as it is in salads. Grow four or five plants per growing-bag.

Although not as attractive or colourful as the vegetables mentioned above, you may also wish to try other suitable kinds such as salad or spring onions, radishes, dwarf French beans, early dwarf peas and outdoor cucumbers. All do extremely well under this method of cultivation.

Attractive herbs
Culinary herbs are attractive plants and look good on the balcony, roof garden or patio. They deserve to be grown in interesting containers, such as low terracotta pots, bowls or troughs, in modern or classical styles.

Parsley can be grown in special parsley pots with holes in the sides, usually made of terracotta.

Herbs should be grown in a well-drained soil-based potting compost and in a warm sunny spot, although Mint will thrive in semi-shade or complete shade.

Among the most useful culinary herbs is Spearmint *(Mentha spicata)* (Z5). Plant 15cm (6in) apart each way and provide plenty of moisture. Parsley *(Petroselinum crispum)* is among the top-ten culinary herbs. Raise it annually from seeds, thinning the seedlings to 15cm (6in) apart each way.

Sage *(Salvia officinalis)* (Z6) can either be raised from seeds or young plants can be bought. If several plants are to be grown space them 30cm (12in) apart each way. Thyme *(Thymus vulgaris)* (Z5) can also be seed-raised, or young plants bought, setting them 20cm (8in) apart each way if several are to be grown.

Chives *(Allium schoenoprasum)* (Z4) are useful. Buy them in small pots and plant 15cm (6in) apart each way. Every two years the clumps should be lifted and divided in the spring.

Rosemary *(Rosmarinus officinalis)* (Z7) is quite a large evergreen shrub with aromatic foliage and attractive blue flowers, so only one plant will be needed. Grow it in a 30cm (12in) wide tub.

Wild Marjoram or Oregano *(Origanum vulgare)* (Z6) is also an attractive perennial herb with pink flowers in the summer. If several plants are grown, space them 20cm (8in) apart each way.

An interesting evergreen shrub with aromatic foliage is the Sweet Bay *(Laurus nobilis)* (Z6). Grow it as a specimen in a wooden tub, at least 30cm (12in) in diameter. Overwinter it in a greenhouse in areas subjected to hard winters.

Fruits
Various fruit trees can be grown in containers and look good when in flower and when bearing their crops. They deserve to be grown in attractive containers – what better than classical square, wooden, white-painted tubs? Alternatively, consider terracotta pots or tubs in classical styles. The diameter and depth of containers for fruit trees should be 45-60cm (18-24in). Grow the trees in a well-drained soil-based potting compost. Each 'unit' will, of course, be quite weighty, so make sure your balcony or roof garden can take it.

Grow fruits in a sheltered warm sunny position and keep a regular eye on watering, as the compost must not be allowed to dry out. Weekly feeding is required in the summer, using a liquid fertiliser with a high potash content to encourage fruiting. Annual pruning is required, not only to initially train the trees, but also to encourage plenty of fruit-bearing shoots. Pruning techniques vary according to the type of fruit tree and the form in which it is grown, so if you are seriously considering growing fruits in containers it would be sensible to consult a specialist fruit book.

A SELECTION FOR TUBS
Apples are best grown as dwarf bush or dwarf pyramid trees. They should be bought on rootstocks which have a dwarfing influence (your garden centre should be able to advise which trees are on dwarfing rootstocks). If you have space for only one tree, buy a 'family' tree which has been grafted with several different varieties. If you want to grow several apple trees, include several varieties to ensure cross-pollination of the flowers. All must flower at the same time and should be compatible. Again, your garden centre should be able to advise which are the best varieties to grow together. All of these comments also apply to pears.

Cherries are amenable to container growing, too. It is best to choose a self-fertile variety (no other varieties are needed to pollinate it) and it must be on a rootstock which has a dwarfing influence. Grow it as a dwarf bush or pyramid. These comments also apply to plums.

Peaches and nectarines adapt happily to containers and are grown as dwarf bush trees. When these fruits flower there are few if any pollinating insects about so the blossoms have to be pollinated by hand. Using a soft brush, simply dab the centre of each bloom in turn to distribute the pollen.

Citrus fruits grow extremely well in containers and add an exotic touch to a balcony, roof garden or patio. In regions which are subjected to frosts, the trees must be overwintered in a cool but frost-free greenhouse or conservatory; or move them to a light position indoors. Do not allow citrus fruits to become frosted. Oranges are probably the most popular citruses, such as the Seville Orange, *Citrus aurantium,* and the Sweet Orange, *C. sinensis.* They

are grown as dwarf bushes or pyramids. Also exotic-looking, with its large hand-shaped leaves, is the Fig, *Ficus carica,* which is very amenable to tub culture. Again, overwinter it under glass to protect the embryo fruits in areas subjected to frosts.

Grape vines can be grown as standards in tubs. They consist of a single straight stem with all the new shoots being produced at the top to form a kind of head. They grow to about 1.8m (6ft) in height. Each winter all the shoots which form the head are pruned back hard – to within one or two buds of their base. Overwinter them under glass in areas subjected to hard frosts.

Apples and other fruits, when container grown, can be trained into dwarf pyramids (a) and dwarf bush trees (b). Fruit trees are attractive when in flower and fruit and deserve to be grown in attractive containers. They would then make fine patio features